Meditative Moments 60 Scripts for Inner Harmony

GERALDINE BOURGEON

Copyright © 2024 Geraldine Bourgeon

All rights reserved.

ISBN: 979-8-88409-255-6

DEDICATION

To those seeking serenity and embracing the journey within, may these meditative scripts be your guide to a harmonious existence. This book is dedicated to the seekers of inner peace, whose quest for tranquillity inspires the beauty of introspection. May each page resonate with the calming cadence of your soul's whispers. I express gratitude for your presence on this shared path of self-discovery.

CONTENTS

Acknowledgements		vi
How to Use This Book?		vii
Book Structure		ix
1	Abundance	1
2	Body Scan	8
3	Breathing	15
4	Compassion	21
5	Empowering Affirmations	28
6	Gratitude	34
7	Grounding	41
8	Healing	48

CONTENTS

9	Inner Child	55
10	Law of Attraction	61
11	Loving-Kindness	68
12	Meditative Floating	75
13	Morning Ritual	82
14	Nature Connection	89
15	Peace	97
16	Positive Emotions	104
17	Savouring	111
18	Sleep	119
19	Stress Release	127
20	Uplifting Frequencies	134

ACKNOWLEDGMENTS

I am deeply thankful to all my meditation teachers, whose wisdom and insights have illuminated my path to inner peace. Their guidance has been invaluable in shaping the essence of this book.

HOW TO USE THIS BOOK?

Welcome to "Meditative Moments — 60 Scripts for Inner Harmony."

Mindfulness offers a myriad of benefits for mental, emotional, and physical wellbeing. By fostering a non-judgmental awareness of thoughts and feelings, mindfulness provides a powerful tool for stress reduction and anxiety management.

Regular practice has been linked to improved focus and cognitive abilities, enhancing decision-making and problem-solving skills.

Additionally, mindfulness promotes emotional regulation, helping individuals navigate challenging situations with greater ease. Physiologically, it has been associated with reduced blood pressure, improved sleep quality, and overall enhanced resilience.

Beyond the individual, the ripple effects of mindfulness extend to improved relationships, fostering empathy and compassionate communication. Ultimately, mindfulness empowers individuals to navigate the complexities of modern life with greater calm, clarity, and a profound sense of inner peace.

This book caters to a diverse audience: yoga and meditation teachers, mindfulness practitioners, therapists, healers, counsellors, and anyone seeking to use guided meditations for personal growth.

While primarily designed for group sessions, this book is equally valuable for individuals. You can gain instant peace by reading through one of the scripts.

The following section is your gateway to maximising the benefits of these mindfulness scripts.

BOOK STRUCTURE

In this book, you can explore 20 common meditation topics, carefully curated and presented in alphabetical order for easy reach.

Each meditation topic offers a selection of three different script lengths:

- 3-5 minutes
- 8-12 minutes
- 15 minutes

Tailor to Your Needs: Select the meditation topic and script length that aligns with your time constraints and objectives. It's your journey – customise it.

Mindful Pauses: The scripts are intentionally pause-free. Recognising the importance of pauses in mindfulness, I encourage you to add many pauses within the script for a more enriching experience.

Background music: Enhance your sessions further by incorporating background music. Create an immersive experience that fosters a deeper connection to the meditation journey and a space for profound relaxation.

Flexibility: Feel empowered to adapt and modify any part of the meditation to suit your preferences or the preferences of those you guide. Make it your own, and let it resonate with your unique style.

Embark on this journey with the flexibility to tailor each meditation to your specific needs and those of your audience. "Meditative Moments – 60 Scripts for Inner Harmony" is your companion in fostering mindfulness and tranquillity.

1. ABUNDANCE

In the expansive landscape of mindfulness, the concept of abundance unfolds as a profound invitation to shift our perspectives and embrace the richness that life has to offer. Rooted in gratitude and mindful awareness, the practice of cultivating abundance involves recognising and appreciating the multitude of blessings that surround us. Emerging research at the intersection of psychology and mindfulness suggests that intentional engagement with abundance-focused practices can lead to a transformative shift in one's mindset, fostering a greater sense of fulfilment and contentment. By directing attention towards the abundance present in various aspects of life, individuals may experience heightened levels of positive emotions, increased satisfaction, and a deeper connection to the present moment. As we navigate the tapestry of mindfulness, the practice of abundance emerges as a mindful pathway, encouraging individuals to recognise and celebrate the abundant gifts that flow through their lives, fostering a mindset of plenty and enhancing their overall wellbeing.

A Field of Abundance (3-5 minutes)

Begin by finding a comfortable and quiet space where you won't be disturbed. Sit or lie down in a relaxed position, with your spine straight and your hands resting gently on your lap. Take a deep breath in through your nose, and slowly exhale through your mouth. Repeat this a few times until you feel your body starting to relax.

Breathe in through your nose, and exhale through your mouth.

Breathe in through your nose, and exhale through your mouth.

Now, bring your attention to the present moment. Feel the weight of your body against the surface beneath you. Notice any sensations in your body, the warmth, the coolness, or any areas of tension. Allow yourself to let go of any stress or tension as you continue to breathe deeply and slowly.

As you breathe, imagine a warm and golden light surrounding you. This light represents the abundant energy of the universe, full of positivity and prosperity. With each breath, visualise this golden light entering your body, filling you with a sense of peace and contentment.

Focus on your heart centre, the area in the middle of your chest. Envision a glowing ball of light in this space, radiating warmth and love. This is your centre of abundance. Feel the energy expanding from your heart, reaching every corner of your being.

Now, think about the various aspects of abundance in your life — abundance in love, in health, in opportunities, and in wealth. Picture each aspect as a vibrant and colourful flower blooming in a beautiful garden. Imagine these flowers growing taller and stronger with each breath you take.

As you continue to breathe, repeat to yourself:

"I am open to receiving abundance in all areas of my life."

"I attract positivity, prosperity, and opportunities effortlessly."

"Abundance flows to me in unexpected and joyful ways."

Visualise yourself surrounded by a field of abundance, where everything you desire is available to you. See yourself moving through this field with ease, picking the fruits of prosperity that resonate with your goals and dreams.

Take a moment to express gratitude for the abundance in your life. Feel a deep sense of appreciation for the present moment and for the opportunities that lie ahead.

When you're ready, slowly bring your awareness back to the room. Wiggle your fingers and toes, and gently open your eyes. Carry the sense of abundance with you throughout your day, knowing that you are aligned with the positive flow of the universe.

The flow of abundance (8-12 Minutes)

Find a quiet and comfortable place to sit or lie down. Close your eyes and take a deep breath in through your nose, allowing the air to fill your lungs, and exhale slowly through your mouth. Repeat this a few times, feeling the tension leave your body with each breath.

Now, bring your awareness to the present moment. Feel the support of the surface beneath you. Let go of any thoughts or worries, allowing your mind to settle into a state of calm.

Visualise roots extending from the base of your spine, reaching deep into the earth. Feel the grounding energy as these roots connect you to the core of the Earth. Imagine drawing up stability and strength from the earth, allowing it to flow through your body.

Focus on the abundance in your life. Begin by expressing gratitude for the simple things – the air you breathe, the beating of your heart, the opportunities that surround you. Feel a sense of appreciation for the abundance that already exists within you and around you.

Picture a warm, golden light above your head. This light represents the universal energy of abundance. See it flowing down towards you, bathing you in a radiant glow. Feel this energy entering your body, filling every cell with vitality and abundance.

Repeat the following affirmations silently or out loud:

"I am open to receiving abundance."

"I am worthy of all good things."

"Abundance flows to me effortlessly."

Visualise these affirmations manifesting in your life.

Imagine a scene of abundance that resonates with you – it could be a lush garden, a flowing river, or a field of golden wheat. Picture yourself surrounded by this abundance, feeling the joy and fulfilment it brings. Allow this vision to become vivid and real in your mind.

Acknowledge and release any thoughts or beliefs that may be blocking the flow of abundance. Visualise them as clouds drifting away, leaving behind a clear sky. Let go of any feelings of scarcity or limitation.

Open your heart to receive. Imagine a gentle stream of abundance flowing towards you. Picture it in the form of opportunities, blessings, and prosperity. Feel the warmth and fulfilment as you welcome this abundance into your life.

Express gratitude once more, thanking the universe for the abundance that is flowing to you. Feel a deep sense of appreciation for the limitless possibilities that await you.

Slowly bring your awareness back to the present moment. Take a few deep breaths, wiggling your fingers and toes. When you're ready, open your eyes.

Carry the sense of abundance with you throughout your day, knowing that you are connected to the infinite flow of prosperity. You might want to repeat this meditation regularly to reinforce your positive mindset and attract abundance into your life.

Embracing Abundance (15 Minutes)

Begin by finding a quiet and comfortable place to sit or lie down. Close your eyes gently and take a few deep breaths to relax your body and mind.

Bring your attention to the present moment. Feel the connection between your body and the surface beneath you. Ground yourself in the here and now.

Inhale deeply through your nose, allowing your lungs to fill with air. Hold your breath for a moment, and then exhale slowly through your mouth. Repeat this process, letting each breath release tension and stress.

Inhale deeply through your nose for a count of 3, allowing your lungs to fill with air. Hold your breath for a count of 4, savouring the life-giving energy. Then, exhale slowly through your mouth for a count of 5. Repeat this rhythmic process, letting each breath extend over the counted beats, gradually releasing tension and stress.

Inhale for a count of 3. Hold your breath for a count of 4. Then, exhale slowly for a count of 5.

Take a moment to reflect on the abundance already present in your life. What are you grateful for? Acknowledge the positive aspects of your life, big or small.

Envision a beautiful garden filled with vibrant flowers, representing the abundance in your life. Imagine each flower as a symbol of a positive aspect – love, health, opportunities, and prosperity.

Repeat the following affirmations:

"I am open to receiving abundance in all areas of my life."

"I attract positive opportunities effortlessly."

"Abundance flows to me easily and naturally."

Picture yourself surrounded by nature – a forest, beach, or meadow. Feel the abundance of life in the natural world and recognise your connection to it.

Set clear intentions for the abundance you wish to manifest. Whether it's financial prosperity, fulfilling relationships, or personal growth, visualise these intentions becoming a reality.

Identify and release any limiting beliefs about abundance. Imagine these beliefs dissolving like clouds, making way for a mindset of abundance and possibility.

Picture a radiant energy flowing through you, connecting you to the universal flow of abundance. Feel this energy nourishing every aspect of your life.

Embrace a sense of self-love and worthiness. Recognise that you deserve abundance in all areas of your life.

Reflect on the balance between giving and receiving. Acknowledge the joy that comes from both giving and graciously receiving abundance.

Imagine your dreams and desires manifesting with joy and ease. Picture yourself living a life filled with the abundance you have envisioned.

Express gratitude for the abundance that is on its way to you. Feel a sense of appreciation for the unlimited possibilities that lie ahead.

Slowly bring your awareness back to the present moment. Wiggle your fingers and toes, and when you're ready, open your eyes. Carry the feeling of abundance with you into your day.

Practise this meditation regularly to help shift your mindset towards abundance and attract positive energy into your life.

2. BODY SCAN

Within the tapestry of mindfulness practices, the Body Scan meditation stands as a gentle yet transformative thread, weaving attention and awareness through the intricate landscapes of the physical self. Originating from mindfulness-based traditions, the Body Scan involves systematically directing attention to different parts of the body, cultivating a heightened sense of present-moment awareness. Research in the field of contemplative neuroscience reveals the manifold benefits of engaging in regular Body Scan meditations. Studies suggest that this practice can contribute to a deeper understanding and acceptance of bodily sensations, fostering a mind-body connection that is integral to overall wellbeing. Furthermore, the Body Scan has been associated with reduced levels of stress, improved sleep quality, and a greater capacity for managing chronic pain. As we embark on this journey of mindfulness, the Body Scan emerges as a valuable tool, inviting individuals to explore the intricate nuances of their physical experiences and cultivate a more harmonious relationship with the body.

Mindful Body Scan (3-5 minutes)

Find a comfortable seated or lying position. Close your eyes gently and take a few deep breaths. Inhale slowly, allowing your chest and abdomen to expand, and exhale fully, releasing any tension or stress. Let go of any thoughts or distractions, and bring your attention to the present moment.

Begin by focusing on your breath. Notice the sensation of the breath as it enters and leaves your body. Feel the rise and fall of your chest and the expansion and contraction of your abdomen. Take a few moments to centre yourself with each breath.

Shift your attention to your feet. Feel the sensations in your toes, the soles of your feet, and your heels. Notice any warmth, coolness, or tingling. Take a few breaths here, allowing any tension in your feet to dissolve with each exhale.

Now, direct your awareness to your lower legs. Feel the weight of your calves and the muscles around your shins. Notice any areas of tension or relaxation. Inhale, sending your breath to any tight spots, and exhale, releasing any stress or discomfort.

Bring your attention to your pelvic area. Feel the contact between your body and the surface beneath you. Notice any sensations in your hips, pelvis, and buttocks. Allow your breath to soften and relax this area.

Shift your focus to your abdomen. Feel the gentle rise and fall with each breath. Move up to your chest, noticing the expansion and contraction of your ribcage. Take a moment to acknowledge any emotions present in this area without judgment.

Shift your awareness to your hands. Feel the sensation in your fingers, palms, and the back of your hands. Move up to your forearms and elbows. Allow any tension to melt away as you continue to breathe deeply.

Bring your attention to your shoulders. Notice if there is any tightness or tension. With each breath, let your shoulders relax and drop away from your ears. Continue to your neck, releasing any stiffness.

Finally, focus on your head and face. Feel the muscles in your jaw, cheeks, and forehead. Relax any tension in your temples. Soften your gaze, and let your facial muscles unwind. Take a few breaths to fully relax your entire head.

Now, take a moment to scan your entire body from head to toe. Notice the sensations, the areas of relaxation, and any remaining areas of tension. Allow your breath to flow through your body, promoting a sense of calm and wellbeing.

As you conclude this body scan meditation, express gratitude for the time you've dedicated to your wellbeing. When you're ready, gently open your eyes, bringing a sense of mindfulness and relaxation into the rest of your day.

Body Scan Serenity (8-12 Minutes)

Begin by finding a comfortable position, either sitting or lying down. Close your eyes gently and take a few deep breaths, inhaling through your nose and exhaling through your mouth. Allow each breath to bring you into the present moment.

Start by focusing on your breath. Notice the sensation of the breath as it enters and leaves your body. Feel the rise and fall of your chest and the expansion and contraction of your abdomen. Take a few moments to centre yourself with each breath.

Shift your attention to your feet. Feel the sensations in your toes, the soles of your feet, and your heels. Notice any warmth, coolness, or tingling. Take a few breaths here, allowing any tension in your feet to dissolve with each exhale.

Now, direct your awareness to your lower legs. Feel the weight of your calves and the muscles around your shins. Notice any areas of tension or relaxation. Inhale, sending your breath to any tight spots, and exhale, releasing any stress or discomfort. Continue to move up through your thighs.

Bring your attention to your pelvic area. Feel the contact between your body and the surface beneath you. Notice any sensations in your hips, pelvis, and buttocks. Allow your breath to soften and relax this area.

Shift your focus to your abdomen. Feel the gentle rise and fall with each breath. Move up to your chest, noticing the expansion and contraction of your ribcage. Take a moment to acknowledge any emotions present in this area without judgment.

Shift your awareness to your hands. Feel the sensation in your fingers, palms, and the back of your hands. Move up to your forearms and elbows. Allow any tension to melt away as you continue to breathe deeply. Feel the energy flowing through your arms.

Bring your attention to your shoulders. Notice if there is any tightness or tension. With each breath, let your shoulders relax and drop away from your ears. Continue to your neck, releasing any stiffness. Imagine any tension melting away, leaving your shoulders and neck feeling light and free.

Finally, focus on your head and face. Feel the muscles in your jaw, cheeks, and forehead. Relax any tension in your temples. Soften your gaze, and let your facial muscles unwind. Take a few breaths to fully relax your entire head.

Now, take a moment to scan your entire body from head to toe. Notice the sensations, the areas of relaxation, and any remaining areas of tension. Allow your breath to flow through your body, promoting a sense of calm and wellbeing.

As you conclude this body scan meditation, express gratitude for the time you've dedicated to your wellbeing. When you're ready, gently open your eyes, bringing a sense of mindfulness and relaxation into the rest of your day.

Body Scan Relaxation (15 Minutes)

Begin by finding a comfortable position, either sitting or lying down. Close your eyes gently and take a few deep breaths. Inhale deeply through your nose, allowing the breath to fill your lungs, and exhale slowly through your mouth, releasing any tension.

Bring your attention to your breath. Feel the natural rhythm of your inhales and exhales. Allow each breath to ground you in the present moment, creating a sense of calm and relaxation.

Shift your awareness to your feet. Feel the connection between your feet and the ground. Notice any sensations - warmth, coolness, or tingling. With each breath, let go of any tension in your feet, inviting a sense of rootedness.

Direct your attention to your lower legs. Feel the weight of your calves and the muscles around your shins. Inhale, imagining the breath travelling through your legs, and exhale, releasing any tightness. Continue this journey up through your thighs, inviting a deep sense of relaxation.

Bring your focus to your pelvic area. Notice the support beneath you. Allow your breath to flow naturally, soothing any tension in your hips, pelvis, and lower back. Feel a sense of stability and ease.

Shift your attention to your chest. Feel the rise and fall of your breath. Bring awareness to your heart centre. With each breath, invite a sense of openness and compassion. Acknowledge any emotions present without judgment.

Extend your awareness to your hands and arms. Feel the energy flowing through your fingertips. Inhale, allowing the breath to travel down your arms, and exhale, releasing any holding. Sense a gentle flow of relaxation through your entire upper body.

Bring attention to your shoulders. Notice any tension residing there. Inhale deeply, lifting your shoulders towards your ears, and exhale, allowing them to melt down. Continue to your neck, releasing any tightness. Feel a cascade of relaxation through your shoulders and neck.

Focus on your head and face. Soften your jaw, unclenching your teeth. Relax the muscles around your eyes and forehead. Inhale, inviting a sense of clarity, and exhale, releasing any lingering tension. Allow your entire head to be light and at ease.

Take a moment to scan your entire body. Notice the interconnectedness of each part. Breathe into any areas that may still hold tension, allowing your breath to promote a sense of harmony and balance throughout your entire being.

As you conclude this body scan meditation, express gratitude for the time and intention you've dedicated to your wellbeing. Take a few deep breaths, and when you're ready, gently open your eyes, carrying this sense of mindfulness and relaxation into the rest of your day.

3. BREATHING

At the heart of mindfulness practice lies the rhythmic dance of breath, an ancient and foundational technique that transcends cultural boundaries. Mindful breathing, a cornerstone of contemplative traditions, invites individuals to harness the power of the breath as a focal point for heightened awareness and presence. Emerging research in neuroscience and mindfulness highlights the profound impact of intentional and mindful breathing on mental and physical wellbeing. Studies suggest that regular engagement in mindful breathing practices can lead to a reduction in stress levels, improved emotional regulation, and increased attentional clarity. Moreover, intentional breathwork has been associated with enhanced respiratory function, promoting a sense of calmness and relaxation. As we delve into the transformative journey of mindfulness, the simple yet profound act of mindful breathing stands as a gateway to the present moment, offering a sanctuary for individuals to anchor themselves amidst the ebb and flow of life's experiences.

Mindful Breathing (3-5 minutes)

Begin by finding a comfortable seated position, whether on a chair or cushion. Sit with your back straight and your hands resting on your knees.

Close your eyes gently and bring your attention to your breath. Notice the natural flow of your breath, the rise, and fall of your chest or the sensation of the breath as it enters and leaves your nostrils.

Take a deep, intentional breath in, and as you exhale, release any tension or stress you may be carrying. Let it melt away with each breath out.

Now, shift your focus to the present moment. Inhale slowly, counting to four. Hold your breath for a moment, and then exhale, counting to six. Repeat this cycle for a few breaths, allowing each breath to ground you in the here and now.

As you continue to breathe mindfully, notice any thoughts that may arise. Acknowledge them without judgment and gently bring your focus back to your breath. Your breath is your anchor to the present moment.

Now, let go of the counting and simply observe your breath. Notice the cool sensation as you inhale and the warmth as you exhale. Feel the rhythmic pattern of your breath, a natural and calming cadence.

If your mind begins to wander, gently guide it back to the breath. You are here, in this moment, connected to the simple and profound act of breathing.

Take a moment to express gratitude for each breath, and for the life it sustains. Inhale positivity, exhale any negativity.

As we conclude this mindful breathing meditation, slowly bring awareness back to your surroundings. When you're ready, gently open your eyes.

May the peace cultivated in this practice stay with you throughout your day.

Breathing Awareness (8-12 minutes)

Begin by finding a comfortable position, either sitting or lying down. Allow your spine to straighten, shoulders to relax, and hands to rest comfortably. Close your eyes gently.

Take a moment to settle into the present moment, letting go of any distractions. Feel the support beneath you, connecting with the surface you're resting on.

Now, bring your attention to your breath. Notice the natural rhythm of your breath. The inhalation, the brief pause, and the exhalation. Observe the gentle rise and fall of your chest or the expansion and contraction of your abdomen.

As you breathe in, be aware of the cool sensation of the air entering your nostrils. And as you breathe out, notice the warmth of the breath as it leaves your body.

Allow your breath to guide you into a state of deep relaxation. Inhale slowly for a count of four, hold your breath for a moment, and exhale for a count of six. Continue this pattern, letting each breath deepen your sense of calm and presence.

As you settle into the flow of your breath, bring your awareness to the sensations in your body. Notice any areas of tension or discomfort. With each exhale, release that tension, allowing it to dissolve into the air.

Now, shift your focus to the expansion of your breath. Feel the breath filling your lungs, expanding your chest, and nourishing your body with each inhalation. With each exhale, imagine releasing any stale air, any negativity, leaving your body.

As you continue to breathe, let go of any need to control the breath. Allow it to flow naturally, like gentle waves lapping at the shore.

If your mind begins to wander, gently redirect it to the breath. Picture your thoughts as clouds passing by in the sky of your mind, without judgment. Bring your attention back to the breath, your anchor in this moment.

As you become more attuned to your breath, sense the

interconnectedness of your body and breath, the dance of life unfolding within you.

Now, for the next few moments, let go of any specific focus. Simply be present with your breath. Allow the breath to be a mirror reflecting the stillness within.

As we bring this breathing awareness meditation to a close, take a few deep breaths, slowly bringing awareness back to your surroundings. Wiggle your fingers and toes, gently reawakening your body.

When you're ready, open your eyes. Carry this sense of mindful breathing and awareness with you into the rest of your day.

May your breath be a constant reminder of the peace that resides within you.

Breathing Relaxation (15 minutes)

Begin by finding a comfortable position, either sitting or lying down. Close your eyes gently, allowing the outside world to fade away.

Take a deep breath in, fill your lungs with fresh air, and exhale, releasing any tension or stress you may be holding onto. Repeat this a few times, feeling the soothing rhythm of your breath.

Now, bring your attention to the natural flow of your breath. Feel the rise and fall of your chest or the gentle expansion and contraction of your abdomen.

As you breathe in, imagine inhaling a calming, golden light. Picture this light filling your entire being with tranquillity. As you exhale, visualise releasing any worries or tightness, letting them dissolve into the air.

Allow your breath to guide you into a state of deep relaxation. Inhale slowly for a count of five, hold your breath for a moment, and exhale for a count of seven. Continue this pattern, letting each breath deepen your sense of calm and relaxation.

Now, bring your awareness to your body. Scan for any areas of tension or discomfort. With each exhale, consciously release and let go of that tension. Feel your body becoming lighter and more at ease with each breath.

As you continue to breathe, imagine a wave of relaxation washing over you with each inhale and exhale. Picture this wave starting at your toes, gradually moving up through your legs, torso, and arms, until it envelops your entire body in a cocoon of serenity.

Shift your focus to the sounds around you – the gentle rhythm of your breath, any ambient sounds in the environment. Allow these sounds to further deepen your state of relaxation, becoming part of the soothing symphony of this moment.

If your mind begins to wander, gently guide it back to the breath. Picture any distracting thoughts as leaves floating down a stream, carried away by the current of your breath.

Now, let go of any specific focus on the breath. Allow your breath to return to its natural, effortless rhythm. Simply be present in this moment, letting go of the need to control or manipulate anything.

As you rest in this stillness, visualise a serene and peaceful place. It could be a beach, a forest, or any place that brings you a sense of tranquillity. Picture yourself there, surrounded by the calming energy of the environment.

For the next few moments, bask in this feeling of complete relaxation and inner peace.

As we gradually bring this breathing relaxation meditation to a close, become aware of your surroundings. Feel the support beneath you, gently wiggle your fingers and toes.

Take a few deep breaths, slowly bringing awareness back to your body.

When you're ready, open your eyes. Carry this sense of deep relaxation with you for the rest of your day.

May you move forward with a heart full of peace and a mind free of tension.

4. COMPASSION

In the vast landscape of mindfulness, the practice of compassion stands as a luminous beacon, illuminating the path towards a more empathetic and interconnected existence. Rooted in ancient wisdom and embraced by contemporary contemplative traditions, the cultivation of compassion involves extending benevolence not only to others but also to oneself. Research in psychology and neuroscience underscores the profound impact of compassion practices on mental and emotional wellbeing. Studies suggest that engaging in regular compassion-focused mindfulness can lead to increased levels of positive emotions, enhanced resilience in the face of adversity, and improved overall mental health. Furthermore, the ripple effects of compassion extend beyond individual wellbeing, contributing to the creation of supportive and empathetic communities. As we traverse the landscapes of mindfulness, the practice of compassion emerges as a transformative force, inviting individuals to open their hearts to the suffering of others and themselves, fostering a more compassionate and harmonious world.

Nurturing Compassion (3-5 minutes)

Begin by finding a comfortable seated position. Close your eyes and take a few deep breaths, allowing the tension to melt away from your body.

Inhale deeply through your nose, feeling the air fill your lungs. Exhale slowly through your mouth, releasing any tension or stress. Repeat this process a few times, letting each breath anchor you in the present moment.

Bring your attention to the sensations in your body. Start from the top of your head, and slowly scan down to your toes. Notice any areas of tension or discomfort. As you breathe out, imagine releasing that tension, allowing it to dissolve with each breath.

Place your hands over your heart. Feel the warmth and gentle rhythm of your heartbeat. Imagine a soft, golden light emanating from your heart centre. With each breath, visualise this light expanding, filling your entire chest with warmth and compassion.

Bring to mind a moment when you experienced difficulty or made a mistake. Instead of dwelling on the negative emotions, offer yourself kindness and understanding. Repeat silently, "May I be free from suffering. May I be happy. May I be at peace."

Picture someone you care about deeply. It could be a friend, family member, or even a pet. Visualise them in your mind's eye, experiencing joy and happiness. Extend the wish for compassion to them, saying, "May you be free from suffering. May you be happy. May you be at peace."

Now, broaden your focus to include all beings on this planet. Envision a world filled with compassion and understanding. As you inhale, imagine drawing in the suffering of the world. As you exhale, send out waves of love, compassion, and healing. Repeat, "May all beings be free from suffering. May all beings be happy. May all beings be at peace."

Take a moment to express gratitude for this time of self-reflection and compassion. When you're ready, slowly bring your awareness back to the present moment. Wiggle your fingers and toes, and gently open your eyes.

Remember, compassion is a gift you can give to yourself and others. Carry this sense of warmth and understanding with you as you go about your day.

Universal Compassion (8-12 Minutes)

Inhale deeply, feeling the breath fill your lungs, and exhale slowly, letting go of any tension. Repeat this a few times until you feel grounded and centred in the present moment.

Visualise roots extending from the base of your spine, reaching down into the Earth. Feel the grounding energy as you connect with the core of the Earth. Sense the stability and support that comes from this connection.

Shift your focus to your heart centre. Imagine a radiant light, a soft and compassionate glow residing within. With each breath, allow this light to expand, enveloping your entire being in a warm embrace of love and understanding.

Bring to mind moments when you've faced challenges or made mistakes. Instead of judgment, offer yourself compassion. In your mind, say, "I am worthy of love and understanding. May I be free from suffering, may I be happy, may I be at peace."

Extend your compassion to those in your immediate surroundings – friends, family, neighbours. Picture them in your mind, and wish them well: "May you be free from suffering, may you be happy, may you be at peace."

Envision your compassion reaching beyond your immediate circle. Picture people from different walks of life, diverse backgrounds, and cultures. Extend your compassionate wishes to them: "May all beings everywhere be free from suffering, may all beings be happy, may all beings be at peace."

Imagine connecting with the natural world. Envision the trees, animals, rivers, and skies. Feel a sense of unity with all living things, recognising the interdependence of life. Offer your compassion to the entire ecosystem.

Picture waves of compassion emanating from your heart, creating a ripple effect that extends far and wide. See these waves touching and healing the hearts of those who need it most, spreading love and understanding across the world.

Sit in stillness for a few moments, feeling the expansiveness of your compassion. Notice any sensations or emotions that arise. Embrace them with an open heart.

Gently bring your awareness back to the present moment. Express gratitude for the compassion you've cultivated. Know that this compassion is a gift that can continue to grow and resonate within you and beyond.

A Compassionate Heart (15 Minutes)

Begin by taking a few deep breaths, inhaling through your nose and exhaling through your mouth. Feel the connection between your breath and the present moment.

Bring your awareness to your body. Notice any areas of tension or discomfort. With each breath, allow the tension to dissolve, creating space for relaxation and ease.

Picture a radiant light in the centre of your chest. This light represents your compassionate heart. As you breathe, visualise this light growing brighter, expanding with each breath, filling your entire body.

Acknowledge any emotions present within you. Without judgment, allow these emotions to be. Embrace them with the warmth of your compassionate heart, understanding that it's okay to feel and that your emotions are valid.

Bring to mind a situation where you may have been hard on yourself. Hold this situation in your awareness and offer yourself words of kindness. Repeat silently, "May I be kind to myself. May I be free from suffering. May I be at peace."

Expand your focus to someone you care about deeply. Visualise them in your mind and extend your compassionate wishes to them: "May you be happy, may you be healthy, may you be safe, may you be at peace." Feel the loving energy flowing from your heart to theirs.

Envision faces of people you may not know personally – strangers in your community or around the world. Send them wishes of compassion and wellbeing: "May you be free from suffering, may you be happy, may you be at peace."

Bring to mind someone with whom you've had challenges. As difficult as it may be, extend compassion to them: "May you be free from suffering, may you find peace and understanding."

Imagine roots extending from your body, anchoring you to the Earth. Feel the grounding energy as you connect with the Earth's wisdom and stability. Sense the interconnectedness of all life.

Expand your compassion to encompass all beings on Earth. Picture a world filled with understanding, empathy, and love. Extend your wishes for global wellbeing: "May all beings be free from suffering, may all beings be happy, may all beings be at peace."

Focus on your breath and the shared breath of all living beings. With each inhale, draw in the essence of compassion. With each exhale, send out waves of love and understanding, contributing to the collective energy of compassion.

Sit in quiet reflection, allowing the resonance of compassion to linger. Notice any shifts in your emotions or perspectives. Embrace the stillness with a compassionate heart.

Express gratitude for this time of deep connection and compassion. Acknowledge the love within your heart. Embrace yourself with gratitude and self-love.

Slowly bring your awareness back to the present moment. Wiggle your fingers and toes. When you're ready, open your eyes, carrying the warmth of compassion with you into the world.

As you go about your day, carry the essence of compassion with you. Notice opportunities to extend kindness and understanding to yourself and others. Know that your compassionate heart has the power to create positive change in the world.

5. EMPOWERING AFFIRMATIONS

In the realm of mindfulness, empowering affirmations stand as potent instruments, capable of shaping the landscape of one's thoughts and beliefs. Rooted in the understanding that the mind plays a pivotal role in shaping our experiences, affirmations become a mindful practice of self-dialogue aimed at fostering positivity and empowerment. Research in psychology and mindfulness suggests that regularly incorporating empowering affirmations into one's routine can lead to a positive shift in mindset, increased self-esteem, and enhanced resilience in the face of challenges. By consciously choosing and repeating affirmations that resonate with personal strengths and aspirations, individuals engage in a transformative dialogue with themselves, fostering a mindset conducive to growth and self-empowerment. As we journey through the realms of mindfulness, the practice of empowering affirmations emerges as a mindful tool, empowering individuals to cultivate a positive and resilient inner narrative that can positively influence their perceptions and experiences.

Blossoming Presence (3-5 minutes)

Take a moment to find a comfortable position, either sitting or lying down. Close your eyes gently, and let your attention turn inward. Inhale deeply through your nose, exhale slowly through your mouth, allowing any tension to melt away.

Repeat the following affirmation:

"I am a beacon of positivity."

Visualise a radiant light at the centre of your chest, glowing brighter with each breath. See this light expanding, casting a warm and positive glow throughout your entire being. Feel the uplifting energy radiating from your core.

"I am a creator of joy."

Picture a garden within your mind. Imagine vibrant flowers blooming, representing moments of joy. Sense the fragrance and beauty surrounding you as you affirm your ability to create and nurture happiness.

"I am in harmony with the rhythm of life."

Envision yourself dancing in rhythm with the natural flow of life. Feel the energy of each step aligning with the universal beat. Sense the effortless harmony as you move through the dance, gracefully connected to the pulse of existence.

"I am grounded in this present moment."

Imagine roots extending from your body, anchoring you to the present. Feel the stability and support of these roots as you affirm your connection to the here and now. Sense the calm and centred presence within.

As you gently bring your awareness back to the present, carry the positive energy and affirmations with you. Take a moment to appreciate the warmth and light you've cultivated within. When you're ready, open your eyes, knowing that this brief burst of affirmation has set a positive tone for your day.

Crafting Dreams (8-12 Minutes)

Find a quiet space where you can sit or lie down comfortably. Close your eyes gently, and take a moment to connect with your breath. Inhale deeply through your nose, feeling the air fill your lungs, and exhale slowly through your mouth, releasing any tension.

As you settle into this tranquil space, become aware of the present moment. Feel the support beneath you, and let go of any worries. Allow the outside world to fade away as your focus turns inward.

Repeat the following affirmation:

"I am a source of boundless creativity."

As you repeat this affirmation, imagine a canvas before you. Visualise vibrant colours and shapes emerging on this canvas, reflecting the infinite well of creativity within you. See the canvas transform into a masterpiece, symbolising the endless possibilities that lie within your creative spirit.

"I embrace change as a natural part of life."

Envision a flowing river, representing the ever-changing nature of life. As you affirm your acceptance of change, picture yourself navigating the gentle currents with ease. Feel the water's calming embrace, recognising that change can be a beautiful and transformative journey.

"I am aligned with the rhythm of the universe."

Imagine standing beneath a celestial sky, surrounded by stars and planets. Sense the cosmic energy flowing through you, aligning your essence with the vast universe. Feel the interconnectedness of all things and the harmony of your being with the cosmic dance.

"I radiate love and compassion."

Picture a warm, golden light expanding from your heart. Visualise this light enveloping you and extending outward, touching the hearts of those around you. Sense the energy of love and compassion creating a soothing and harmonious atmosphere.

As you gently bring your awareness back to the present, take a moment to appreciate the serenity within. Know that this state of harmony, creativity, acceptance, and love is always accessible to you. Carry these positive vibrations with you as you open your eyes, returning to the world with a renewed sense of inner balance.

Whispers of Strength (15 Minutes)

In this meditation, we will repeat affirmations, and in addition, we will incorporate visualisation. This act of visualising will transform the affirmations into vivid experiences that can have a positive impact on your mindset and overall wellbeing.

Find a comfortable space where you can sit or lie down. Close your eyes gently and take a few deep breaths to centre yourself in this present moment. Allow the outside world to fade away as you turn your attention inward. Feel the support of the surface beneath you and let go of any tension in your body.

As you settle into this space, become aware of your breath. Inhale deeply through your nose, feeling the air fill your lungs, and exhale slowly through your mouth, releasing any stress or worry. With each breath, allow yourself to sink deeper into relaxation.

"I am strong, capable, and resilient."

As you repeat this affirmation, envision a powerful, radiant light within you. Imagine it growing brighter with each repetition, symbolising the strength that resides in your core. Feel the warmth and assurance of this inner strength enveloping you.

"I bounce back from challenges, stronger than before."

Picture yourself like a resilient tree swaying in the wind but remaining firmly rooted. Visualise challenges as the wind, and with each affirmation, see your branches flex and sway, adapting to the winds of change while maintaining your inner stability.

"I rise above challenges with grace and ease."

Envision challenges as stepping stones in your path. With each affirmation, visualise yourself effortlessly stepping over these stones, transcending obstacles. See yourself moving forward, gaining strength and wisdom from each experience.

"I attract positive energy and radiate it outward."

Imagine a vibrant, glowing aura around you. With each affirmation, see this aura expanding and becoming more luminous. Feel the positivity radiating from your being, creating a harmonious and uplifting atmosphere around you.

"I have the courage to face and conquer my fears."

Picture your fears as shadows. As you affirm your courage, visualise a radiant light dispelling these shadows. Sense the warmth and bravery emanating from within, allowing you to confront and overcome any fears that may arise.

"I love and accept myself unconditionally."

Envision a gentle, nurturing light embracing you. With each affirmation, see this light filling every part of your being with love and acceptance. Feel the warmth of self-love permeating your thoughts, emotions, and physical body.

Now, gently open your eyes. Take a moment to acknowledge the transformative journey you've just embarked upon. The affirmations and visualisations you've embraced have ignited a powerful resonance within.

Carry this newfound strength, resilience, and positivity with you into the world. Whether you continue your day or transition to rest, remember the radiant light, the resilient tree, the stepping stones, and the glowing aura.

You are a beacon of positive energy, courage, and self-love. Embrace the empowerment you've cultivated within, and let it radiate outward, enriching your mindset and overall wellbeing.

6. GRATITUDE

In the expansive realm of mindfulness, the practice of gratitude serves as a luminous thread, weaving through the tapestry of awareness and fostering a profound shift in perspective. Grounded in the recognition of life's blessings, both big and small, cultivating gratitude becomes a transformative journey towards a more mindful and appreciative existence. Emerging research in psychology and contemplative science underscores the myriad benefits of incorporating gratitude practices into our daily lives. Studies suggest that regularly expressing and reflecting on gratitude can lead to increased levels of positive emotions, improved overall wellbeing, and a greater sense of life satisfaction. Moreover, the practice has been associated with reduced symptoms of depression and anxiety, fostering emotional resilience in the face of life's challenges. As we navigate the landscapes of mindfulness, the practice of gratitude beckons individuals to embrace a mindful appreciation for the richness of their experiences, encouraging a harmonious dance with the present moment.

Cultivating Gratitude (3-5 minutes)

Begin by finding a comfortable and quiet space where you can sit or lie down. Close your eyes and take a few deep breaths, inhaling slowly through your nose and exhaling through your mouth. Allow any tension in your body to release with each breath.

Start by bringing your awareness to the present moment. Feel the support beneath you, whether you're sitting or lying down. Take a moment to appreciate the connection between your body and the surface below.

Inhale deeply, allowing your lungs to fill with air, and exhale slowly, letting go of any stress or worries. Repeat this a few times until you feel centred and grounded.

Shift your attention to your body. Begin at the top of your head and slowly move down, acknowledging each part of your body. As you focus on each area, express gratitude for its function and the experiences it allows you to have.

Feel grateful for your eyes that allow you to see the beauty around you, your ears that enable you to hear the world, your heart that beats tirelessly, and every other part of your body that contributes to your wellbeing.

Bring your attention back to your breath. With each inhalation, imagine breathing in gratitude. Visualise the air filling you with a warm and glowing light of appreciation. As you exhale, release any tension or negativity.

Continue to breathe in gratitude and exhale negativity, creating a cycle of positivity flowing through your body and mind.

Take a moment to think about specific people, experiences, or things you are grateful for in your life. It could be a supportive friend, a loving family member, a fulfilling job, or even simple pleasures like a warm cup of tea or a beautiful sunset.

Allow these images to fill your mind, and as you reflect on each one, let the feeling of gratitude wash over you.

Now, expand your gratitude beyond your immediate circle. Think about the interconnectedness of all living beings. Express gratitude for the Earth that sustains us, for the sun that provides warmth, and for the countless people around the world contributing to the wellbeing of humanity.

Feel a sense of connection and unity with the world, recognising the abundance of blessings that surround us.

Gently bring your awareness back to the present moment. Wiggle your fingers and toes, slowly becoming aware of your surroundings. When you're ready, open your eyes.

Carry the feelings of gratitude with you throughout your day, allowing them to positively influence your thoughts and actions. Remember that gratitude is a practice, and the more you cultivate it, the more joy and contentment you may experience in your life.

Abundant Living (8-12 Minutes)

Begin by finding a quiet and comfortable space. Sit or lie down, allowing yourself to settle into a relaxed position. Close your eyes gently, and take a few deep breaths to centre yourself in the present moment.

Start by focusing on your breath. Inhale deeply, and as you exhale, let go of any tension or stress. With each breath, imagine roots extending from your body, connecting you to the earth below. Feel grounded and supported by the energy of the earth.

Shift your attention to your senses. Notice the sounds around you, whether they are distant or near. Acknowledge the temperature of the air against your skin. Be aware of any scents that may be present. Take a moment to appreciate the richness of the sensory experiences that surround you.

Bring your awareness to your body. Start with your toes and gradually move upward, thanking each part of your body for its unique role. Express gratitude for your feet that carry you, your hands that create and connect, and your heart that beats with the rhythm of life.

Take a moment to appreciate the health and vitality that your body provides.

Focus on your breath once again. Inhale deeply, and as you exhale, visualise a warm and radiant light spreading through your body. This light represents the gratitude you carry within. With each breath, let this light expand, filling every cell and fibre of your being.

Feel the energy of gratitude flowing through you, uplifting and renewing.

With your heart open, reflect on the blessings in your life. Consider the people, experiences, and opportunities that have enriched your journey. Allow a deep sense of gratitude to well up within you as you recognise the abundance that surrounds you.

Take your time to savour these moments of reflection.

Embrace the challenges and difficulties you've faced. Recognise them as opportunities for growth and learning. Express gratitude for the strength and resilience that these challenges have cultivated within you.

As you acknowledge the lessons learned, let go of any lingering negativity, and appreciate the transformative power of adversity.

Extend your gratitude beyond yourself. Envision a circle of light expanding outward, touching the lives of your loved ones, your community, and the entire world. Picture this light connecting all beings, fostering a sense of unity and compassion.

Feel the interconnectedness of all living things, and express gratitude for the shared human experience.

Project your awareness into the future. Envision the path ahead filled with opportunities, growth, and joy. Express gratitude for the abundance that is yet to come, trusting that the universe has more blessings in store for you.

Embrace the anticipation of a future filled with gratitude.

Gently bring your awareness back to the present moment. Wiggle your fingers and toes, slowly reconnecting with your surroundings. Carry a sense of gratitude with you as you go about your day, knowing that the practice of abundant living is a continuous journey.

When you're ready, open your eyes, feeling refreshed and filled with gratitude for the abundant life that surrounds you.

May your journey of abundant living be guided by gratitude and positivity.

Feeling Blessed (15 Minutes)

Begin by finding a quiet and comfortable space. Sit or lie down in a relaxed position, and close your eyes gently. Take a few deep breaths to centre yourself in the present moment.

Envision yourself standing in a radiant garden. This garden represents the vast landscape of your life. Notice the colours, scents, and textures around you. With each step, feel the ground beneath your feet, knowing that this garden is a reflection of your journey.

Imagine roots extending from the soles of your feet, reaching deep into the Earth. Feel the grounding energy as you connect with the core of the Earth. Sense the stability and support that Mother Earth provides, allowing you to stand strong in gratitude.

Bring your awareness to the present moment. Acknowledge the gift of being alive. Feel gratitude for the breath that flows effortlessly through you, for the beating of your heart, and for the unique experience of this moment.

Explore each of your senses. Notice the sounds around you, the sensations on your skin, the aromas in the air, and any tastes lingering in your mouth. Express gratitude for the richness of these sensory experiences that contribute to your understanding of the world.

Focus on your breath. Inhale deeply, allowing the air to fill your lungs, and exhale slowly, releasing any tension. With each breath, feel gratitude for the life-sustaining force within you. Recognise that each breath is a reminder of the abundance of life.

Bring to mind a recent challenge or difficulty. Instead of resisting, embrace it with gratitude. Reflect on the lessons learned and the strengths gained. Express thanks for the opportunities that challenges bring to grow and evolve.

Visualise the people in your life who bring love and support. See their faces and feel the warmth of their presence. Express gratitude for the connections that nourish your soul. Consider reaching out to someone later to share your appreciation.

Imagine yourself surrounded by the beauty of nature — majestic mountains, flowing rivers, and lush forests. Feel a deep connection to the natural world. Express gratitude for the Earth and its ability to inspire and rejuvenate.

Acknowledge the creative force within you. Whether through art, writing, or any form of expression, express gratitude for the ability to create and bring something new into the world. Recognise the power of your unique creative energy.

Visualise a stream of golden light flowing towards you, carrying abundance in all its forms. Feel this abundance permeating every aspect of your life – health, love, opportunities, and joy. Express deep gratitude for the overflowing blessings.

Find gratitude in moments of silence. Allow yourself to appreciate the stillness between thoughts, the quiet spaces that allow for introspection and peace. In this silence, feel a profound connection to your inner self.

Reflect on the knowledge and wisdom you've gained throughout your journey. Express thanks for the experiences that have expanded your understanding and shaped your perspective. Embrace the continual process of learning and growth.

Embrace the mystery of the unknown. Acknowledge that life unfolds in unexpected ways. Express gratitude for the anticipation of what's to come, trusting that every twist and turn is part of your unique and purposeful journey.

Shift your focus inward. See yourself with eyes of love and appreciation. Express gratitude for your resilience, uniqueness, and the journey you're on. Recognise the strength within you to navigate the complexities of life.

Gently bring your awareness back to the present moment. Wiggle your fingers and toes, slowly returning to your surroundings. Carry the radiant gratitude with you as you move forward, knowing that your journey is illuminated by the light of appreciation.

Take a final deep breath and open your eyes, feeling refreshed and filled with radiant gratitude for the abundant tapestry of your life.

7. GROUNDING

In the vast expanse of mindfulness, the practice of grounding emerges as a stabilising force, inviting individuals to anchor themselves in the present moment amidst the whirlwind of life's demands. Rooted in both ancient contemplative traditions and modern therapeutic approaches, grounding techniques aim to reconnect individuals with the present reality, fostering a sense of stability and balance. Research in psychology and mindfulness highlights the profound impact of grounding practices on emotional regulation and overall wellbeing. Techniques such as mindful breathing, body awareness, and grounding exercises have been shown to reduce symptoms of anxiety and stress, promoting a greater sense of calmness and resilience. By consciously engaging with the sensations of the body and the immediate environment, individuals cultivate a mindful presence that acts as a foundation for navigating life's challenges. As we traverse the landscapes of mindfulness, the practice of grounding becomes a grounding anchor, allowing individuals to remain rooted in the richness of the present moment, ultimately fostering a more centred and grounded existence.

Finding Your Centre (3-5 minutes)

Welcome to this guided grounding meditation. Let's begin by finding a comfortable seated position, with your spine straight and your hands resting on your knees or in your lap. Take a deep breath in through your nose, and exhale slowly through your mouth. Feel the tension leaving your body as you release the breath.

Take a few moments to focus on your breath. Inhale deeply, feeling the air fill your lungs, and exhale, letting go of any tension. As you breathe in, visualise positive energy entering your body, and as you exhale, release any stress or negativity. Continue this rhythmic breathing, allowing yourself to become fully present in this moment.

Imagine roots extending from the base of your spine, reaching down into the Earth. Visualise these roots growing deeper and grounding you firmly to the Earth's core. Feel the supportive and nurturing energy rising up through these roots, bringing a sense of stability and strength.

Shift your attention to the physical sensations in your body. Starting from the top of your head, slowly scan down through your body. Notice any areas of tension or discomfort. As you breathe, imagine sending your breath to these areas, allowing them to relax and release any stress. Move down through your neck, shoulders, chest, and all the way to your toes.

Bring your attention to the present moment. Notice the sounds around you, the sensation of your breath, and the feeling of your body in the present space. Allow any thoughts or distractions to come and go, gently bringing your focus back to your breath and the present moment.

Imagine yourself in a serene natural setting, perhaps a meadow, a beach, or a forest. Feel the texture of the ground beneath you. Picture the colours, smells, and sounds of this place. As you stand or sit in this peaceful environment, absorb the grounding energy from the Earth, feeling a deep connection to nature.

Take a moment to reflect on the things you are grateful for in your life. Express gratitude for the Earth's support, for the strength you find within yourself, and for the present moment. Let this gratitude fill your heart with warmth and appreciation.

Slowly bring your awareness back to the room. Wiggle your fingers and toes, and gently open your eyes. Take a moment to appreciate the grounded and centred energy you've cultivated during this meditation.

As you go about your day, carry this sense of grounding with you, knowing that you can return to this peaceful state whenever you need to find your centre. Thank you for joining this guided grounding meditation. May you move forward with a grounded and tranquil spirit.

Being Rooted in Tranquillity (8-12 Minutes)

Welcome to this guided grounding meditation. Find a comfortable seated or lying position, allowing your body to relax and settle into the space around you. Close your eyes gently, and let's begin by taking a deep, cleansing breath in through your nose and exhaling slowly through your mouth.

Bring your awareness to your breath. Inhale deeply, filling your lungs with fresh air, and exhale, releasing any tension or stress. With each breath, allow your body to sink into relaxation, feeling the gentle rise and fall of your chest.

Shift your attention to the physical sensations in your body. Starting from your toes, gradually move your awareness up through your legs, torso, arms, and head. Notice any areas of tension or discomfort. Without judgment, simply observe these sensations, allowing them to soften and release as you breathe.

Imagine yourself in a serene forest. Picture tall, majestic trees surrounding you. Feel the earth beneath your feet, covered in soft moss. As you stand or sit in this peaceful grove, visualise roots extending from the soles of your feet, growing deep into the soil. Envision these roots connecting with the vibrant energy of the Earth, grounding you in stability and strength.

Feel the energy from the Earth rising up through your roots. Visualise it as a warm, golden light that fills your entire body. Allow this energy to cleanse and rejuvenate you, bringing a sense of balance and harmony. Sense the connection between your energy and the Earth's energy, creating a reciprocal flow of support.

Bring your focus back to your breath. As you inhale, imagine drawing in the revitalising energy from the Earth. As you exhale, release any remaining tension, allowing it to dissolve into the ground. With each breath, sense a deepening connection to the Earth's calming and stabilising energy.

Reflect on the interconnectedness of all life. Express gratitude for the Earth's unwavering support. Feel a sense of unity with the natural world and acknowledge the strength and resilience within yourself. Allow gratitude to fill your heart, creating a deep sense of inner peace.

Sit in stillness, embracing the quietude of the present moment. Feel the grounding energy within you and around you. Let go of any thoughts or distractions, fully immersing yourself in the tranquillity of this meditation.

Gently bring your awareness back to the room. Wiggle your fingers and toes, and when you're ready, slowly open your eyes. Carry the grounded energy you've cultivated into the rest of your day, knowing that you can return to this place of tranquillity whenever needed.

Thank you for joining in this guided grounding meditation. May you move forward with a renewed sense of balance, strength, and peace.

Nurturing Connection (15 Minutes)

Welcome to this guided grounding meditation. Find a comfortable position, either sitting or lying down. Close your eyes gently, and let's begin by taking a deep, rejuvenating breath in through your nose, holding it for a moment, and then exhaling slowly through your mouth. Allow your breath to guide you into a state of relaxation.

Bring your attention to your physical body. Begin by noticing any areas of tension or discomfort. As you breathe, consciously release this tension, allowing each breath to create a sense of spaciousness and ease throughout your body. Feel the weight of your body sinking into the support beneath you.

Shift your focus to your breath. Imagine each inhale drawing in revitalising energy from the universe, and each exhale releasing any stagnant or negative energy. Visualise the breath as a gentle wave, cleansing and purifying your entire being. Let the breath be a conduit for connection and balance.

Envision yourself in a beautiful, tranquil garden. The sun is warm, and a gentle breeze carries a sense of peace. As you walk through the garden, notice the variety of plants and flowers. Find a comfortable spot to sit or stand. Feel the ground beneath you, whether it's soft grass or cool earth. Sense the support and stability it offers.

Now, visualise a ball of golden light hovering above your head. This light represents universal energy, and as it descends slowly, feel it connecting with the top of your head. Allow this energy to flow through your body, bringing a sense of balance and alignment. As it reaches your feet, imagine roots extending deep into the Earth, securing you to its nurturing core.

To reinforce your grounding experience, repeat the following grounding affirmations to yourself silently or out loud:

"I am rooted in the present moment."

"I am supported by the Earth's energy."

"I am connected to the source of tranquillity within me."

Allow these affirmations to resonate within, fostering a deep sense of security and calm.

Engage your senses. Notice the temperature of the air on your skin, the scents around you, and any sounds in the environment. Embrace the sensory richness of the present moment. Feel the interconnectedness between your senses and the Earth, enhancing your grounding experience.

Express gratitude for the Earth's support and the grounding energy you've cultivated. As you exhale, release any remaining tension or concerns, allowing them to dissipate into the Earth. Feel a lightness and spaciousness within, knowing you are grounded and connected.

Gently bring your awareness back to your surroundings. Wiggle your fingers and toes, and when you're ready, slowly open your eyes. Take a moment to integrate the grounding energy into your daily life. Carry this sense of connection and tranquillity with you as you move through the rest of your day.

Thank you for joining in this guided grounding meditation. May you walk forward with a deep sense of connection, stability, and peace.

8. HEALING

In the expansive landscape of mindfulness, the journey of healing unfolds as a transformative odyssey, inviting individuals to navigate the intricate pathways of physical, emotional, and spiritual restoration. Rooted in ancient traditions and embraced by contemporary therapeutic approaches, mindfulness plays a crucial role in the healing process. Research in psychology and integrative medicine highlights the profound impact of mindfulness on various aspects of healing, from reducing stress-related symptoms to promoting emotional wellbeing. Mindfulness-based interventions, such as meditation and mindful breathing, have been associated with improvements in chronic pain, anxiety, and depression. By fostering a gentle awareness of the present moment, individuals embark on a healing journey that encompasses both self-compassion and acceptance. As we traverse the realms of mindfulness, the practice of healing becomes a mindful embrace, allowing individuals to reconnect with their innate capacity for resilience and restoration, promoting a holistic sense of wellbeing.

Healing Light Meditation (3-5 minutes)

Begin by finding a comfortable and quiet space where you won't be disturbed. Sit or lie down in a relaxed position, allowing your body to settle into a comfortable posture. Take a few deep breaths, inhaling through your nose, and exhaling through your mouth.

Start by bringing your awareness to the present moment. Feel the connection between your body and the surface beneath you. Imagine roots extending from your body into the earth, anchoring you and providing a sense of stability. With each breath, imagine drawing in energy from the earth, filling your body with healing light.

Shift your focus to your breath. Inhale deeply through your nose, allowing your lungs to fill with fresh, revitalising air. As you exhale, release any tension or negativity. Visualise each breath as a source of healing energy, circulating through your body and promoting a sense of calm and wellbeing.

Bring your attention to different parts of your body, starting from your toes and gradually moving up to the top of your head. As you focus on each area, imagine a warm, healing light enveloping it. If you encounter any areas of tension or discomfort, visualise the light gently dissolving any blockages or stress, leaving that part of your body relaxed and at ease.

Allow yourself to acknowledge and express any emotions that may be present. If there is pain or sorrow, let it come to the surface without judgment. Imagine these emotions as clouds passing by in the sky, gradually dissipating and making way for a clearer, lighter state of being. As you release these emotions, invite feelings of love and compassion to fill the space within you.

Repeat positive affirmations to reinforce a sense of healing and wellbeing:

"I am deserving of love and healing."

"I am strong, resilient, and at peace."

Let these affirmations resonate within you, allowing them to guide your thoughts towards positivity and self-compassion.

Gradually bring your awareness back to the present moment. Wiggle your fingers and toes, and take a few more deep breaths. When you feel ready, gently open your eyes.

Consistent practice contributes to a sense of inner peace and healing over time.

Guided Healing Journey (8-12 Minutes)

Begin by finding a quiet and comfortable space. Close your eyes and take a few moments to settle into a relaxed posture. Breathe deeply, inhaling through your nose and exhaling through your mouth.

Focus on your breath, allowing it to become slow and steady. Inhale positivity and exhale any tension or negativity. Imagine a golden light surrounding you, creating a protective cocoon of healing energy.

Bring your awareness to your heart centre. Visualise a radiant light at the core of your chest, glowing with warmth and compassion. With each breath, feel this light expanding, filling your entire being with love and healing energy.

Imagine a gentle stream of water flowing through you. As it moves, visualise it carrying away any pain, sorrow, or emotional burdens. Picture these emotions dissolving into the water, leaving you feeling lighter and more at peace.

Shift your focus to your physical body. Starting from your toes, imagine a wave of soothing energy moving upward through each part of your body. Feel the warmth and relaxation as the healing energy flows, releasing any tension or discomfort along the way.

Envision yourself in a serene natural setting, surrounded by lush greenery or a calming body of water. Feel the healing energy of nature infusing your being. Visualise the sun's rays or the gentle breeze carrying away any lingering negativity.

Repeat positive affirmations related to healing:

"I am deserving of health and happiness."

"I release what no longer serves me, inviting healing into my life."
Let these affirmations resonate deeply within you.

Picture a bright, healing light above you. See it descending slowly, surrounding you like a comforting blanket. As it envelops you, imagine any physical or emotional wounds being bathed in this warm light, promoting rapid and profound healing.

Extend your hands in front of you, palms facing outward. Imagine sending healing energy from your heart through your hands. Envision this energy flowing outward, touching and positively influencing the world around you. Recognise the interconnectedness of healing and the power of positive intention.

Shift your focus to gratitude. Reflect on aspects of your life that bring joy and positivity. Express thanks for the healing energy you've received and for the potential for continued growth and wellbeing.

Gently bring your awareness back to the present moment. Wiggle your fingers and toes, and take a few deep breaths. When you're ready, open your eyes, carrying the sense of healing and peace with you into your day.

Finding Your Healing Space (15 Minutes)

Find a quiet and comfortable space. Sit or lie down, ensuring you won't be disturbed. Take a moment to set the intention for healing, allowing yourself to be open to the process.

Begin by focusing on your breath. Inhale deeply through your nose, allowing your lungs to fill with air. Exhale slowly through your mouth, releasing any tension. With each breath, envision a calming energy entering your body and exhaling any stagnant energy.

Visualise roots extending from the base of your spine, anchoring you to the Earth. Feel the stability and support these roots provide, connecting you to the grounding energy of the Earth beneath you.

Slowly shift your attention to different parts of your body. As you scan, notice any areas of tension or discomfort. Send your breath and awareness to these areas, encouraging them to release and relax. Picture a gentle, healing light soothing each part of your body.

Acknowledge any emotional burdens you carry. Visualise these burdens as stones in a backpack on your shoulders. With each breath, release the stones one by one, allowing them to fall away. Embrace forgiveness for yourself and others.

Imagine standing by a serene lake. Dip your toes into the healing waters, feeling a cool, revitalising energy rising through your body. Allow this energy to cleanse away any emotional residue, leaving you refreshed and renewed.

Envision a series of colourful energy circles aligned along your spine. Starting from the base, visualise each chakra glowing with its unique colour. See the energy flowing smoothly, creating a harmonious balance from the base to the crown.

Picture yourself in a tranquil garden filled with vibrant flowers. Each flower represents an aspect of your wellbeing. As you explore, visualise these flowers blooming, radiating health and vitality. Feel the garden nurturing your entire being.

Reflect on moments in your life that may require self-compassion. Offer kindness and understanding to yourself. Visualise a warm, golden light surrounding your heart, fostering self-love and acceptance.

Create an inner sanctuary within your mind. This can be a place of safety and peace. Explore the details of this sanctuary, knowing that you can return here whenever you need to find solace and healing.

Repeat affirmations focused on healing and wholeness, reinforcing positive intentions:

"I am a vessel of healing energy."

"My body, mind, and spirit are in perfect harmony."

Imagine a brilliant light above you, representing a universal source of healing energy. Allow this light to enter your being, permeating every cell with radiant, transformative energy. Feel a sense of oneness with the healing power of the universe.

Gradually bring your awareness back to the present moment. Wiggle your fingers and toes, feeling the connection with your physical body. Recognise that the healing energy you've cultivated remains with you, integrated into your being.

Express gratitude for the healing journey you've undertaken. Acknowledge the strength within you and the potential for ongoing healing. When you're ready, gently open your eyes, carrying the sense of wholeness with you into your day.

As you go about your day, carry the intention of healing with you. Embrace each moment as an opportunity for growth and restoration. Remember that the journey towards healing is ongoing, and you have the power to nurture your wellbeing.

9. INNER CHILD

In the realm of mindfulness, the concept of the Inner Child stands as a tender and transformative exploration into the depths of one's emotional landscape. Rooted in psychology and embraced by mindfulness practices, the Inner Child represents the collection of early experiences, emotions, and vulnerabilities that shape the core of our being. Mindfulness invites individuals to embark on a compassionate journey of self-discovery, reconnecting with and nurturing the Inner Child. Research in psychology and trauma-informed mindfulness suggests that acknowledging and embracing the Inner Child can be a powerful step towards healing and self-compassion. Mindfulness practices that focus on gentle self-exploration and inner attunement provide a nurturing space for individuals to heal past wounds and cultivate a more balanced and integrated sense of self. As we navigate the intricate terrain of mindfulness, the exploration of the Inner Child becomes a poignant process, fostering self-love, resilience, and a profound understanding of the interconnectedness between our past and present selves.

Nurturing Your Inner Child (3-5 minutes)

Begin by finding a comfortable and quiet space where you won't be disturbed. Sit or lie down in a relaxed position. Close your eyes and take a few deep breaths, allowing yourself to let go of any tension.

Start by bringing your awareness to the present moment. Feel the support beneath you, whether it's the chair, cushion, or floor. Take a moment to connect with the sensation of being grounded.

Picture yourself in a beautiful, serene place – a place that feels safe and comforting. It could be a meadow, a beach, a forest, or any place that resonates with you. Notice the colours, the smells, and the sounds around you.

In this safe space, imagine a younger version of yourself – your inner child. Picture them standing or playing nearby. Observe the child's appearance, the clothes they are wearing, and the expression on their face. Approach your inner child with open arms and a warm smile.

Gently let your inner child know that you are here, present, and ready to connect. Assure them that they are loved, accepted, and safe. Take a moment to embrace your inner child, allowing the warmth and love to flow between you. Feel the connection strengthening with each breath.

Ask your inner child if there is anything they need or want to share with you. Listen attentively and respond with love and understanding. Offer words of comfort and reassurance. Affirm that you are committed to taking care of and nurturing your inner child.

As you slowly bring your awareness back to the present moment, express gratitude for the connection you've made with your inner child. Take a few deep breaths, gradually becoming aware of your surroundings.

Whenever you feel the need for comfort or connection with your inner child, return to this meditation. Remember that this inner child is a part of you, deserving of love and compassion.

Rediscovering Joy Within (8-12 Minutes)

Find a quiet and comfortable space where you can sit or lie down. Close your eyes and take a few deep breaths, allowing yourself to relax and be fully present in this moment.

Begin by grounding yourself in the present. Feel the support beneath you, the surface you're sitting or lying on. Become aware of the sensations in your body and gently release any tension with each exhale.

Imagine yourself in a serene garden. This garden is safe, filled with vibrant flowers, lush greenery, and a gentle breeze. Picture this space in as much detail as you can, creating a sanctuary within your mind.

In this garden, envision a small, playful version of yourself. Your inner child is excited to see you. Notice the innocence, curiosity, and joy in their eyes. Approach your inner child, and as you get closer, see them light up with joy and anticipation.

Engage in play with your inner child. Explore the garden together. Run, laugh, and embrace the sense of freedom. Take note of the things that bring joy to your inner child – the simple pleasures that may have been forgotten over the years.

Sit down with your inner child and have a heart-to-heart conversation. Ask them how they're feeling and listen without judgment. Share words of reassurance, telling your inner child that you are here for them, ready to provide love and support.

Open your arms and invite your inner child into a warm embrace. Feel the exchange of love and comfort between you. As you hold them, let the healing energy flow, mending any wounds or hurts from the past.

Speak affirmations of self-love to your inner child:

"You are worthy of love and acceptance just as you are."

"You are deserving of all the good things life has to offer."

Repeat these affirmations with sincerity, allowing them to resonate deeply within you.

Now, engage in a heartfelt conversation with your present self, repeating after me:

"I am worthy of love just as I am."

"My uniqueness is my strength."

"I embrace the unconditional love within me."

Express these affirmations sincerely and repeat them, allowing the positive words to resonate deeply within your being. Feel the transformative power of self-love as it embraces both your present self and your inner child, nurturing a profound sense of acceptance and joy.

"I am worthy of love just as I am."

"My uniqueness is my strength."

"I embrace the unconditional love within me."

Express gratitude for this precious connection with your inner child. Feel the warmth and love radiating within you. Visualise your inner child integrating with your present self, becoming a source of strength, joy, and creativity.

Slowly bring your awareness back to the room. Take a few deep breaths, gently wiggle your fingers and toes, and when you're ready, open your eyes.

Remember, this meditation is a tool you can return to whenever you want to reconnect with the joy and innocence of your inner child, and to embrace a journey of self-discovery.

The Inner Child Sanctuary (15 Minutes)

Begin by finding a comfortable position, either sitting or lying down. Close your eyes and take a few deep breaths, inhaling positivity and exhaling any tension or negativity. Allow yourself to be fully present in this moment.

Visualise roots extending from your body into the Earth, anchoring you in the present moment. Feel the supportive energy of the Earth beneath you. Take a few moments to scan your body, releasing any tension with each exhale.

Picture yourself in a peaceful and serene place, your own Inner Child Sanctuary. This can be a cozy room, a beautiful garden, or any place where you feel safe and loved. Explore the details of this sanctuary, noticing colours, textures, and sounds.

As you explore, come across a younger version of yourself. Observe them playing, laughing, or sitting quietly. Approach your inner child with open arms and a warm smile. Greet them with love and acceptance.

Engage in a conversation with your inner child. Ask them how they feel and what they need. Listen attentively, offering understanding and reassurance. Share words of comfort and let your inner child express their thoughts and feelings freely.

Invite your inner child to embrace you. Feel the warmth and love exchanged between you two. As you embrace, imagine a healing light surrounding both of you, washing away any pain or sadness. Sense the renewal and transformation happening within.

Repeat affirmations of empowerment and self-love:

"I am deserving of love."

"I embrace my inner child with compassion."

"I am capable and resilient."

Feel the positive energy of these affirmations resonating within.

Visualise your inner child merging seamlessly with your present self. Feel the integration of their innocence, joy, and authenticity into your current being. Sense a newfound strength and wholeness within.

Express gratitude for this journey of healing and connection. Slowly bring your awareness back to the present moment. Wiggle your fingers and toes, take a few deep breaths, and when you're ready, gently open your eyes.

Allow this meditation to be a source of healing and empowerment as you continue your journey of self-discovery and self-love.

10. LAW OF ATTRACTION

In the expansive landscape of mindfulness, the concept of attraction reveals itself as a nuanced exploration into the interplay of thoughts, emotions, and energies. Rooted in mindfulness traditions and the understanding that our thoughts shape our experiences, the practice of mindful attraction involves intentional focus on positive and affirmative aspects of life. Research in psychology and mindfulness suggests that the principles of attraction, when approached mindfully, can influence one's mindset and overall wellbeing. By cultivating positive thoughts, fostering gratitude, and maintaining a present awareness, individuals may experience a shift in their vibrational energy, influencing their perceptions and interactions with the world. Mindful attraction is not merely about external desires but involves a deeper alignment with one's authentic self and the present moment. As we navigate the realms of mindfulness, the practice of mindful attraction becomes an exploration of the profound connection between our inner states of being and the magnetic forces that shape our experiences in the world.

Manifesting Abundance (3-5 minutes)

Welcome to this guided meditation on the Law of Attraction. Find a comfortable seated or lying position, close your eyes, and take a deep breath in through your nose, allowing your abdomen to expand. Exhale slowly through your mouth, releasing any tension or stress.

As you continue to breathe deeply and rhythmically, bring your awareness to the present moment. Feel the weight of your body on the surface below you, grounding yourself in this space and time.

Now, imagine a warm, golden light surrounding you. This light represents the powerful energy of the Law of Attraction, a force that draws similar energies together. Envision this golden light flowing through every cell of your being, filling you with positivity and possibility.

As you breathe, visualise yourself in a serene and beautiful place, surrounded by the manifestations of your desires. Picture in vivid detail what success, happiness, and abundance look like for you. Imagine the sensations, sounds, and emotions associated with these manifestations.

Now, focus on gratitude. Bring to mind three things you are grateful for in this moment. It could be the people in your life, the opportunities you've been given, or the simple joys that surround you. Feel the warmth of gratitude filling your heart.

In the realm of the Law of Attraction, gratitude is a powerful magnet for attracting more of what you want. Express your gratitude to the universe for the blessings in your life, and trust that more abundance is on its way.

As you continue to breathe, let go of any doubts or limiting beliefs that may be holding you back. Imagine them dissipating like smoke, leaving space for a renewed sense of self-belief and confidence in the Law of Attraction.

Now, bring your attention to your thoughts. Recognise the power they hold in shaping your reality. Affirm positive statements about yourself and your life. Repeat after me silently or out loud:

"I am a powerful creator of my reality."

"I attract positivity and abundance effortlessly."

"My thoughts and intentions shape my destiny."

Feel the energy of these affirmations resonating within you, aligning your thoughts with the vibrations of the universe.

Now, take a moment to set a clear intention for what you want to attract into your life. Be specific and positive. See it as if it's already happening. Trust in the process and believe that the universe is conspiring to bring your desires to fruition.

As we begin to conclude this meditation, take a few deep breaths, slowly bringing your awareness back to the present moment. Wiggle your fingers and toes, and when you're ready, gently open your eyes.

Carry this sense of positive energy and belief with you throughout your day, knowing that you are a co-creator of your reality, and the universe is working in harmony with your desires.

Namaste.

Unleashing Your Inner Power (8-12 Minutes)

Welcome to this guided meditation on the Law of Attraction. Find a quiet and comfortable space where you won't be disturbed. Sit or lie down, close your eyes, and take a deep breath in through your nose, exhaling slowly through your mouth. Let go of any tension, and allow yourself to be fully present in this moment.

As you continue to breathe deeply, imagine a radiant ball of golden light hovering above your head. This light represents the universal energy of attraction, a force that aligns with your thoughts and intentions. Feel this light descending slowly, surrounding your body and permeating every cell with positivity and possibility.

Now, focus on your breath. Inhale deeply, allowing your abdomen to expand, and exhale fully, releasing any stress or worries. With each breath, imagine yourself becoming more attuned to the frequency of the Law of Attraction.

Visualise a serene landscape before you. It's a canvas of infinite possibilities. As you explore this landscape in your mind's eye, notice the vibrant colours, the sounds of nature, and the sensations of joy and abundance that surround you.

Now, bring your attention to your heart centre. Feel the warmth and energy radiating from this space. This is the centre of your emotions and intentions. Imagine a small seed within your heart, representing your deepest desires. With each beat, this seed sends out ripples of energy, attracting similar vibrations from the universe.

Picture in vivid detail the life you want to create. Envision success, love, and abundance. See yourself achieving your goals, surrounded by positivity, and living the life of your dreams. Engage all your senses in this visualisation, making it as real and tangible as possible.

As you hold this vision, express gratitude for the manifestations that have already come into your life. Feel a sense of appreciation for the journey and the lessons learned. Gratitude is a powerful amplifier of the Law of Attraction.

Now, let go of any doubts or limiting beliefs. Imagine them

dissolving like mist, leaving behind a clear space for the abundance that awaits you. Repeat after me, either silently or out loud:

"I release all doubts and fears. I am deserving of abundance."

"I trust in the flow of the universe, knowing that what I seek is seeking me."

"I am a powerful co-creator of my reality, and I attract positive experiences effortlessly."

Feel the energy of these affirmations resonating within you, aligning your thoughts and intentions with the frequency of the Law of Attraction.

Take a moment to set a clear and specific intention for what you want to manifest. See it as already happening, and believe in the magic of the universe conspiring to make it a reality.

As we begin to conclude this meditation, gradually bring your awareness back to the present moment. Wiggle your fingers and toes, take a few deep breaths, and when you're ready, gently open your eyes.

Carry this sense of empowerment, gratitude, and belief with you as you go about your day. You are a co-creator of your reality, and the universe is always working in harmony with your intentions.

Namaste.

Calling to the Universe (15 Minutes)

Welcome to this 15-minute guided meditation on the Law of Attraction. Find a quiet and comfortable space where you won't be disturbed. Sit or lie down, close your eyes, and take a moment to centre yourself. Inhale deeply through your nose, and exhale slowly through your mouth, releasing any tension in your body.

As you continue to breathe, imagine a soft, golden light surrounding you. This light is the pure energy of the universe, the source of all creation. Feel it gently entering your body with each breath, filling you with warmth, positivity, and the essence of the Law of Attraction.

Now, let's bring awareness to the present moment. Feel the ground beneath you, supporting you. Be present with your breath, allowing it to guide you into a state of relaxation and receptivity.

Visualise yourself standing at the edge of a vast, tranquil lake. The surface of the water is calm and reflective, mirroring the limitless potential within you. This lake represents the reservoir of your desires and intentions.

As you stand by the lake, set the intention to release any resistance or limiting beliefs that may be blocking the flow of abundance in your life. Imagine these limiting beliefs as stones in your pockets. With each breath, release them one by one into the lake, watching as they disappear beneath the surface.

Now, let's journey deeper into the power of your thoughts. Imagine your mind as a garden. Notice the thoughts that arise – are they seeds of positivity, or weeds of doubt? With each inhale, visualise planting seeds of intention in the fertile soil of your mind. See these seeds growing into vibrant, beautiful flowers that represent your dreams and desires.

As you focus on these flowers, become aware of the emotions they evoke. Allow yourself to feel the joy, gratitude, and fulfilment as if your desires have already manifested. The Law of Attraction responds to the energy of your emotions, so immerse yourself in the positive feelings of abundance.

Now, let's enter a state of deep gratitude. Think of three things you are grateful for right now. Feel the warmth of gratitude expanding within your heart. Gratitude is a powerful magnet that attracts more of what you appreciate into your life.

As you continue to breathe, imagine a radiant beam of light extending from your heart centre into the universe. This beam of light connects you to the infinite possibilities that await. Visualise this connection strengthening, allowing the energy of the universe to flow through you and support your intentions.

Take a moment to affirm your beliefs in the Law of Attraction. Repeat after me, either silently or out loud:

"I am a powerful creator of my reality."

"I attract abundance effortlessly."

"My thoughts and intentions shape my destiny."

Feel the resonance of these affirmations vibrating within you, aligning your energy with the universal flow.

Now, in this state of heightened awareness, set a specific and clear intention for what you want to manifest. See it with vivid detail, as if it's happening right now. Trust that the universe is conspiring to bring your desires into reality.

As we begin to conclude this meditation, gradually bring your awareness back to the present moment. Wiggle your fingers and toes, take a few deep breaths, and when you're ready, gently open your eyes.

Carry this sense of empowerment, gratitude, and belief with you as you move through your day. You are a co-creator of your reality, and the universe is always responding to your thoughts and intentions.

Namaste.

11. LOVING-KINDNESS

In the realm of mindfulness, one profound practice that has garnered increasing attention for its transformative effects is loving-kindness meditation. Rooted in ancient contemplative traditions, this practice extends beyond the boundaries of self-awareness to cultivate a profound sense of compassion and goodwill towards oneself and others. Recent research in the field of neuroscience and psychology has unveiled compelling evidence supporting the positive impact of loving-kindness meditation on mental wellbeing. Studies suggest that regular engagement in this meditative practice can lead to heightened levels of positive emotions, improved mood, and decreased symptoms of anxiety and depression. Moreover, the practice has been associated with enhanced empathy and a more resilient emotional response to life's challenges. As we explore the profound journey into the realms of mindfulness, the cultivation of loving-kindness emerges as a powerful avenue for fostering a compassionate and interconnected way of being.

Cultivating Compassion (3-5 minutes)

Find a quiet and comfortable space where you won't be disturbed. Sit or lie down in a relaxed position. Close your eyes if you feel comfortable doing so.

Begin by taking a few deep breaths in and out. Inhale deeply, allowing your lungs to fill with air, and exhale fully, letting go of any tension. Feel the connection between your body and the ground beneath you.

Bring your awareness to yourself. Imagine a warm and gentle light surrounding your body, a light of pure love and kindness. With each breath, allow this light to grow brighter, wrapping you in a cocoon of compassion.

Silently repeat to yourself:

"May I be happy, may I be healthy, may I be safe, may I be at ease."

Feel the warmth of these words permeating your entire being. Allow any judgments or self-criticisms to dissolve in this loving light.

Now, bring to mind someone you love deeply. It could be a friend, family member, or partner. Visualise them in your mind's eye, surrounded by the same warm light of loving-kindness.

Silently repeat:

"May you be happy, may you be healthy, may you be safe, may you be at ease."

Feel the connection and love you have for this person growing stronger with each repetition. Imagine your love reaching out to them and enveloping them in a comforting embrace.

Expand your focus to include someone you may not know very well, perhaps a colleague or acquaintance. Picture them in your mind and extend the same wishes:

"May you be happy, may you be healthy, may you be safe, may you be at ease."

Allow the boundaries of your compassion to widen, embracing a broader circle of humanity.

Finally, expand your loving-kindness to encompass all beings, near and far. Picture the entire world bathed in the light of compassion. Silently repeat:

"May all beings be happy, may all beings be healthy, may all beings be safe, may all beings be at ease."

Feel the interconnectedness of all living things, bound together by the common desire for happiness and wellbeing.

As you conclude this meditation, take a few deep breaths. Slowly bring your awareness back to the present moment, feeling the gentle rise and fall of your breath.

Express gratitude for the love and kindness within you. Carry this feeling of compassion with you throughout your day, allowing it to influence your interactions with others.

When you're ready, gently open your eyes.

The Energy of Loving-Kindness (8-12 Minutes)

Find a quiet and comfortable space. Sit in a relaxed yet alert posture, allowing your hands to rest on your knees and your spine to be straight. Close your eyes gently if it feels comfortable.

Begin by taking a few moments to centre yourself. Inhale deeply through your nose, feeling the breath fill your lungs, and exhale slowly through your mouth, releasing any tension. Allow your breath to return to its natural rhythm.

Direct your attention inward. Visualise a warm and soothing light at the centre of your chest, radiating pure love and kindness. With each breath, let this light expand, enveloping your entire being.

Silently repeat to yourself:

"May I be filled with love and kindness. May I be safe from inner and outer harm. May I be well in body and mind. May I be at ease and happy."

Feel these words resonate within you, cultivating a sense of deep self-compassion.

Now, bring to mind someone in your life whom you care about deeply. Picture them in your mind's eye, and with each breath, extend the warm light of loving-kindness towards them.

Silently repeat:

"May you be filled with loving-kindness. May you be safe from inner and outer harm. May you be well in body and mind. May you be at ease and happy."

Imagine your love and good wishes reaching them, creating a connection of compassion.

Shift your focus to someone you have neutral feelings towards, perhaps a person you encounter in your daily life but don't know well. Picture them in your mind and extend the same wishes:

"May you be filled with loving-kindness. May you be safe from inner and outer harm. May you be well in body and mind. May you be at ease and happy."

Notice how the simple act of extending kindness can transform your perception of others.

Now, bring to mind someone with whom you may have had difficulties or conflicts. Hold them in your awareness, and with an open heart, offer the same wishes:

"May you be filled with loving-kindness. May you be safe from inner and outer harm. May you be well in body and mind. May you be at ease and happy."

Allow any feelings of resentment or negativity to be softened by the light of compassion.

Open your heart even wider, expanding your loving-kindness to include all beings, near and far, known and unknown. Visualise the entire world bathed in the radiant light of compassion.

Silently repeat:

"May all beings be filled with loving-kindness. May all beings be safe from inner and outer harm. May all beings be well in body and mind. May all beings be at ease and happy."

Feel a sense of interconnectedness and shared humanity.

Take a few moments to rest in the energy of loving-kindness. Feel the warmth and openness in your heart. Allow the loving-kindness you've cultivated to nourish your entire being.

As you bring this meditation to a close, take a few deep breaths. Acknowledge the love and kindness within you. Express gratitude for the capacity to generate compassion.

When you're ready, gently open your eyes.

A Journey of Universal Love (15 Minutes)

Begin by finding a comfortable and quiet space. Sit in a relaxed posture with your spine straight, and gently close your eyes.

Take a few deep breaths, inhaling through your nose and exhaling through your mouth. Allow each breath to anchor you to the present moment. Feel the sensation of the breath entering and leaving your body.

Direct your attention inward. Imagine a soft, golden light at the centre of your chest, representing the essence of loving-kindness. As you breathe in, let this light expand, filling every part of your being.

Silently repeat:

"May I be filled with loving-kindness. May I be held in compassion. May I be at peace. May I be truly happy."

Sense the warmth of this light and the tender embrace of self-compassion.

Bring to mind someone you deeply care about – a friend, family member, or a mentor. Picture them in your mind, surrounded by the same golden light of loving-kindness.

Silently repeat:

"May you be filled with loving-kindness. May you be held in compassion. May you be at peace. May you be truly happy."

Feel the connection and shared joy as you extend your well-wishes to them.

Expand your focus to people you encounter in your daily life, perhaps colleagues, neighbours, or strangers you pass by. Visualise them in your mind and offer the same wishes:

"May you be filled with loving-kindness. May you be held in compassion. May you be at peace. May you be truly happy."

Sense the ripple effect of kindness reaching out beyond your immediate circle.

Now, bring to mind someone who may be facing difficulties or challenges. Imagine them surrounded by the golden light of loving-kindness.

Silently repeat:

"May you be filled with loving-kindness. May you be held in compassion. May you be at peace. May you be truly happy."

Send thoughts of strength and support, wishing them ease in their struggles.

Expand your focus even further, envisioning the entire world bathed in the radiant golden light of loving-kindness. Picture people of different cultures, backgrounds, and beliefs living in harmony.

Silently repeat:

"May all beings be filled with loving-kindness. May all beings be held in compassion. May all beings be at peace. May all beings be truly happy."

Feel the collective energy of compassion embracing the world.

Allow the golden light of loving-kindness to flow back to you, absorbing the universal compassion you've cultivated. Sense yourself surrounded by the collective energy of goodwill and understanding.

Take a few moments to simply rest in the energy of loving-kindness. Feel the expansiveness of your heart and the interconnectedness with all living beings.

As you gently bring this meditation to a close, express gratitude for the capacity to cultivate and share loving-kindness. Take a few deep breaths, bringing awareness back to the present moment.

When you're ready, open your eyes with a sense of warmth and openness.

12. MEDITATIVE FLOATING

In the serene waters of mindfulness, the practice of meditative floating emerges as a tranquil voyage into the depths of self-discovery and inner calm. Rooted in the meditative traditions that blend buoyancy with mindfulness, floating experiences provide a unique avenue for individuals to surrender to the gentle embrace of stillness. Research in the fields of psychology and contemplative science suggests that meditative floating can lead to profound states of relaxation, reduced muscle tension, and enhanced mental clarity. The buoyancy of the water creates an environment that encourages a deep letting go, allowing individuals to release physical and mental burdens. As the mind quiets and the body effortlessly floats, individuals may find themselves in a state of profound meditation, cultivating a sense of weightlessness that mirrors the release of emotional and mental burdens. As we embark on the mindful exploration of meditative floating, the experience becomes a gentle surrender, inviting individuals to float effortlessly on the surface of serenity and discover the expansive peace that resides within.

Whispers of Still Waters (3-5 minutes)

Before we begin, find a comfortable and quiet space where you won't be disturbed. Sit or lie down in a relaxed position, close your eyes, and take a few deep breaths to centre yourself. Let's embark on a journey of meditative floating.

Begin by bringing your awareness to your breath. Inhale deeply through your nose, feeling your lungs expand, and exhale slowly through your mouth, releasing any tension or stress. Allow each breath to be a gentle reminder to be present in this moment.

Now, imagine yourself in a tranquil space, surrounded by soft, soothing colours. Picture a vast, calm body of water stretching out before you. It could be an ocean, a lake, or a serene pond. Feel the warmth of the sun on your skin, and sense a gentle breeze caressing your face.

As you stand at the edge of the water, notice a small boat waiting for you. Step into it and feel the support beneath you. This boat represents your journey into relaxation and inner peace.

As you gently push away from the shore, notice how the water beneath you is clear and inviting. With each breath, imagine yourself becoming lighter, as if you are floating effortlessly. Visualise your body becoming weightless, free from any physical constraints.

Allow the boat to guide you further into the centre of the water. Feel a sense of serenity enveloping you, like a soft blanket. Notice the gentle rocking of the boat as it moves with the rhythm of the water, lulling you into a state of tranquillity.

As you continue to float, let go of any thoughts that may arise. Imagine them as clouds passing by in the sky, effortlessly drifting away. Focus on the sensation of floating, surrendering to the stillness within.

Now, turn your attention to the sky above you. Picture it as a vast canvas of endless possibilities. Feel a profound connection to the universe, as if you are a part of something much greater than yourself. Embrace the expansiveness and openness of this moment.

As you float in this serene space, affirm to yourself:

"I am weightless, free, and at peace."

Repeat this affirmation with each breath, allowing it to resonate within you, reinforcing a deep sense of relaxation.

In the next few moments, simply be. Let go of any need to control or understand. Embrace the meditative floating sensation and allow yourself to be fully present in this tranquil experience.

When you are ready to return, slowly bring your awareness back to your physical surroundings. Feel the support beneath you, gently wiggle your fingers and toes, and when you're ready, open your eyes.

Carry the sense of calm and tranquillity from this meditative floating session into your day, knowing that you can return to this inner oasis whenever you need to find peace within.

Celestial Drift (8-12 Minutes)

Find a comfortable and quiet space, sit or lie down, close your eyes, and let's embark on a deeper exploration of meditative floating.

Begin by taking a few moments to settle into your space. Feel the support beneath you and take a deep breath in, allowing your chest to expand, and exhale slowly, releasing any tension. With each breath, feel yourself becoming more present in this moment.

Imagine yourself in a magical garden, surrounded by the soft glow of twilight. The air is filled with a gentle, warm breeze, carrying the soothing scent of blooming flowers. In the centre of this garden, there is a luminous pool of water, inviting you to experience the transformative power of meditative floating.

As you approach the pool, notice the surface of the water is calm and reflective. The moonlight gently dances on its surface, creating a serene and tranquil atmosphere. Step into the water, feeling its temperature perfectly attuned to your comfort.

With each step, sense the water embracing you, supporting your every movement. Gradually, allow yourself to float effortlessly, trusting the water to hold you in its gentle cradle. Feel the sensation of weightlessness as you surrender to the buoyancy of the water.

As you float, become aware of the gentle ripples around you, echoing the subtle movements of your breath. Imagine these ripples as the vibrations of relaxation, spreading tranquillity throughout your being. With each breath, release any lingering tension, allowing it to dissolve into the calming waters.

As you continue to float, notice the reflections on the water's surface. Visualise the reflections as glimpses of your inner self, revealing the beauty and serenity within. Embrace these reflections, acknowledging the depth of peace that resides within your core.

Now, let your mind wander. Imagine a starry sky above, reflecting in the still waters below. Each star represents a moment of tranquillity, a reminder that you are part of the vast cosmic dance of existence. Feel a profound connection to the universe, a sense of oneness with the cosmos.

In this meditative float, grant yourself the gift of timelessness. Let go of the constraints of time and space. Allow the water to cradle you in a cocoon of serenity, transcending the boundaries of the physical world.

As you float in this timeless space, affirm to yourself:

"I am one with the ebb and flow of life."

"I surrender to the rhythm of the universe."

"I find peace in the stillness within."

When you feel ready to return, slowly become aware of your surroundings. Feel the gentle support beneath you, and when you're ready, open your eyes.

Carry the sense of tranquill___ ___ meditative floating journey with you, allowing it to ___ ___ ect of your being. Know that you can retur___ ___ ner peace whenever you choose.

A Celestial Voyage (15 Minutes)

Settle into a comfortable position in a quiet space. Close your eyes, take a few deep breaths, and let's embark on a deep exploration of meditative floating.

Begin by grounding yourself in the present moment. Feel the weight of your body against the support beneath you. Take a deep breath in, allowing the air to fill your lungs, and exhale, releasing any tension.

As you settle into the quietude, envision yourself standing on the shore of a tranquil, secluded lake. The air is filled with the sweet scent of pine trees, and a gentle breeze rustles the leaves. The water before you is crystal clear, reflecting the surrounding nature.

Step into the water, and notice how it embraces you with a perfect balance of warmth and coolness. Feel the water gently caressing your skin as you start to float effortlessly. With each breath, surrender to the sensation of weightlessness, allowing the water to cradle you in a serene embrace.

As you float, let your mind become attuned to the rhythm of the gentle waves. Imagine the sun above you, casting a warm and golden glow. Picture the sunlight dancing on the water's surface, creating a tapestry of shimmering reflections.

Now, let go of any thoughts that may arise. Imagine them as leaves gently floating away from the trees, carried by the current of a peaceful stream. Allow your mind to become as serene as the lake around you.

With each breath, visualise a soft light emanating from within, expanding with every inhale and enveloping you in a cocoon of tranquillity with every exhale. Sense this light spreading through your body, bringing deep relaxation to every muscle and fibre.

As you continue to float, imagine a canopy of stars appearing above you. The night sky unfolds like a cosmic masterpiece, and you find yourself drifting upward, weightless beneath the vast expanse of the universe.

Feel the interconnectedness of all things. Picture the stars as reflections of the countless moments of serenity within you. Embrace the feeling of oneness with the cosmos, a tiny speck in the grand cosmic dance.

In this state of meditative floating, affirm to yourself:

"I am in harmony with the universe."

"I am part of the cosmic flow."

"I am at peace in the vastness of existence."

Allow yourself to linger in this celestial state, drifting through the cosmos, for a few moments. Enjoy the expansive stillness and the gentle dance of the stars.

When you're ready to return, slowly become aware of your breath. Feel the water beneath you, the air around you, and the support beneath your body. With gratitude for this meditative voyage, open your eyes.

Carry the sense of tranquillity and connection with you as you re-enter your day, knowing that you can return to this celestial lake within your mind whenever you seek peace and serenity.

13. MORNING RITUAL

In the art of mindful living, the morning ritual unfolds as a sacred practice, a deliberate and intentional dance with the dawning of each new day. Rooted in the wisdom of ancient traditions and embraced by contemporary mindfulness enthusiasts, the morning ritual serves as a gateway to set a positive tone for the hours ahead. Research in psychology and wellbeing indicates that cultivating a mindful morning ritual can contribute to increased overall life satisfaction and improved mental wellbeing. Whether it involves meditation, gratitude practices, or mindful movement, a purposeful morning ritual becomes a cornerstone for creating a mindful and centred foundation for the day. By engaging in activities that nourish the body, mind, and spirit, individuals can foster a sense of groundedness, clarity, and intention that carries them through the unfolding moments of the day. As we embark on the journey of a mindful morning ritual, it becomes a transformative act, inviting individuals to greet each day with presence, purpose, and a mindful embrace of the possibilities that lie ahead.

Morning Radiance (3-5 minutes)

Take a few moments to settle into a relaxed position, whether you're still lying in bed or sitting comfortably. Close your eyes, take a deep breath in through your nose, and exhale through your mouth. Let go of any tension or stress with each breath.

As you begin your morning ritual, visualise yourself in a tranquil space. The room is filled with soft, warm light, and you feel a sense of peace surrounding you. Take a moment to connect with your breath, inhaling positive energy and exhaling any lingering negativity.

Now, bring your awareness to your body. Feel the gentle warmth of the bed beneath you and the softness of your sheets. Wiggle your fingers and toes, slowly awakening each part of your body. Take a deep breath and stretch your arms overhead, reaching for the sky. As you do, imagine releasing any tightness or stiffness, allowing your body to embrace the new day.

Transition your focus to gratitude. Think about three things you are grateful for today. It could be the warmth of the sunlight, the love of your family, or the opportunities that lie ahead. With each gratitude, feel a sense of warmth and positivity enveloping you.

Now, let's set an intention for the day. Visualise your day unfolding with ease, joy, and fulfilment. See yourself navigating through tasks effortlessly, embracing challenges with a calm and centred mind. Envision positive interactions and a sense of accomplishment at the end of the day.

As you transition from visualisation to physical movement, gently rise from your bed. Feel the support of the floor beneath your feet as you stand tall. Take a moment to express gratitude for the gift of mobility and the ability to start a new day.

Next, move into a simple stretching routine. Reach for the sky, bend forward to touch your toes, and slowly twist from side to side. Feel the energy flowing through your body as you awaken your muscles. With each stretch, let go of any remaining tension, allowing your body to embrace the movement.

Now, pay attention to the sensations around you. Feel the air against your skin, the light streaming through the window, and the comforting softness of your surroundings. Pay attention to any sounds around you. Engage your senses fully in this moment, allowing yourself to be present and attuned to the world around you.

Before you start your day, take a final moment of stillness. Close your eyes and connect with the calm within you. Acknowledge the potential that this new day holds. Take a deep breath in, and as you exhale, open your eyes.

You are now ready to embrace the day ahead with a sense of calm, gratitude, and intention. Carry this positive energy with you throughout your morning and into the rest of your day. Whenever you need a moment of peace, return to this guided meditation to reconnect with your morning ritual.

Awakening Serenity (8-12 Minutes)

Take a moment to find a comfortable position. Adjust your posture until you feel completely at ease, allowing your body to relax and release any tension it may be holding. Begin by acknowledging that this is your sacred time. This is your morning ritual, a time for self-care, reflection, and intentional living. With each breath, allow yourself to sink deeper into the present moment, letting go of the outside world.

Gently close your eyes. Visualise a serene and welcoming space, your own haven of tranquillity. Picture a room filled with soft morning light, a gentle breeze, and the soothing sounds of nature. This is your sanctuary.

Bring your attention to gratitude. Reflect on three things you're grateful for today. Feel the warmth of these thoughts filling your heart, cultivating a sense of appreciation and contentment.

Shift your focus to your breath. Inhale deeply, allowing the air to fill your lungs, and exhale fully, releasing any residual tension. With each breath, envision a wave of calmness washing over you, bringing a renewed sense of energy.

Slowly bring awareness to your body. Start with your toes and gradually move up, thanking each part for its function and strength. Feel the support of the earth beneath you, grounding you in this moment.

Begin to gently stretch your body. Reach your arms overhead, elongate your spine, and twist from side to side. Feel the awakening of your muscles and the energy circulating throughout your being.

Take a moment to set positive intentions for the day. Envision yourself navigating challenges with grace, embracing opportunities, and fostering meaningful connections. See the day unfolding in alignment with your highest aspirations.

Feel the textures, temperatures, and sensations surrounding you, allowing each moment to unfold with mindful awareness.

Take a few moments of stillness. Allow your thoughts to come and go without judgment. Be present with the sounds around you, the feeling of the air on your skin, and the rhythm of your breath.

As you conclude this morning ritual meditation, recognise the gift you've given yourself – the gift of presence, gratitude, and intentional living. Carry this sense of calm and mindfulness with you as you step into the world, knowing that you have set the tone for a positive and fulfilling day.

Open your eyes, bringing the tranquillity of this practice into the rest of your morning. Remember, you have the power to infuse every moment with mindfulness and serenity.

Morning Harmony Awakening (15 Minutes)

Find a comfortable seated position or lie down, allowing your body to sink into relaxation. Close your eyes and take a deep breath in, letting it out with a gentle sigh. Release any tension in your body and begin to settle into this moment.

Bring your awareness to your breath. Inhale deeply through your nose, feeling your chest and abdomen expand. Exhale slowly through your mouth, releasing any stress or worries. Repeat this cycle, allowing each breath to ground you in the present moment.

With each breath, conduct a gentle body scan. Start from your toes, moving up through your legs, torso, arms, and head. Notice any areas of tension and consciously release it with your breath. Feel your entire body becoming a vessel of relaxation.

Picture a vibrant sunrise in your mind's eye. See the sky painted in hues of orange, pink, and gold. Imagine the warmth of the sun's rays gently touching your skin, filling you with a sense of renewal and vitality. Breathe in the energy of this imaginary sunrise, allowing it to invigorate your being.

Envision a lush garden before you. Each flower represents something you are grateful for. Take a stroll through this garden, pausing at each bloom to express your gratitude. Feel the positive energy of appreciation filling your heart.

Repeat a series of positive affirmations about your day:

"I am filled with confidence and positivity."

"I welcome each moment with open arms."

"I trust in my ability to find joy and beauty in every moment, no matter how challenging it may seem."

"I am capable of overcoming any obstacle."

Let these affirmations shape your mindset as you prepare to face the day ahead.

Slowly begin to move your body. Stretch your limbs, wiggle your fingers and toes. Connect with the physical sensations of movement, grounding yourself in the present. As you move, maintain a sense of mindfulness, paying attention to the details of each motion.

Imagine a gentle breeze passing through, clearing away any lingering negativity or doubts. Inhale deeply, visualising this refreshing breeze cleansing your mind, body, and spirit. Exhale, releasing anything that no longer serves you.

Imagine yourself engaging in your morning rituals – whether it's preparing a cup of tea, taking a shower, or getting dressed. Feel the textures, scents, and sensations associated with each activity. Let these rituals become a mindful dance, a symphony of sensory experiences.

Take a moment to set intentions for the day. What qualities do you want to embody? What goals do you wish to pursue? See yourself moving through the day with purpose and presence.

Visualise yourself in a natural setting. Feel the earth beneath your feet or imagine the touch of grass on your skin. Connect with the energy of nature, acknowledging your place in the larger tapestry of life.

As you slowly bring this meditation to a close, express gratitude for this sacred time you've dedicated to yourself. Carry the sense of harmony and mindfulness into your day, knowing that you have laid a foundation for a day filled with peace and purpose.

Open your eyes, returning to the present moment with a renewed sense of clarity and presence. Carry the tranquillity of this morning ritual with you as you step into the world, ready to embrace the day with a heart full of gratitude and a mind centred in peace.

14. NATURE CONNECTION

Amid the hustle and bustle of modern life, the concept of nature connection emerges as a sanctuary for the restless mind, a tranquil haven woven into the fabric of mindfulness. Rooted in the understanding that our wellbeing is intricately linked to the natural world, nature connection practices invite individuals to attune their senses to the rhythmic pulse of the earth. Research in environmental psychology and mindfulness reveals that cultivating a deep connection with nature can lead to a myriad of physical, mental, and emotional benefits. Studies suggest that exposure to natural environments and mindful engagement with the outdoors are associated with reduced stress levels, enhanced mood, and improved cognitive function. Furthermore, nature connection has been linked to increased feelings of awe and interconnectedness, fostering a sense of belonging to something larger than oneself. As we navigate the landscapes of mindfulness, the path of nature connection emerges as a vital thread, inviting individuals to rediscover harmony with the natural world and, in turn, nurture the wellspring of peace and balance within.

Elemental Connection (3-5 minutes)

Find a quiet and comfortable space where you won't be disturbed. Sit or lie down, close your eyes, and take a few deep breaths to centre yourself. As you breathe in, imagine pure, refreshing air filling your lungs. As you exhale, release any tension or stress.

Visualise yourself in a serene natural setting. Picture a lush forest, a tranquil meadow, or a peaceful beach. As you breathe in, feel the essence of this natural place entering your body. Imagine the air is infused with the pure energy of nature.

Inhale deeply, and with each breath, sense the connection growing stronger. Feel the life force of the trees, the grass, or the waves flowing into you. Allow your breath to harmonise with the rhythm of nature around you.

Envision roots extending from the base of your spine, reaching deep into the earth. Picture them anchoring you securely, like the roots of a strong, ancient tree. Feel the support of the earth beneath you, providing stability and strength.

Take a moment to acknowledge the reciprocal relationship with the earth. As you draw energy from the ground, send gratitude and love back to the earth. Sense the exchange of energy, fostering a deep connection with the natural world.

Gradually, bring your awareness to each of your senses. Open your ears to the sounds of nature – birds singing, leaves rustling, or waves crashing. Let these sounds transport you deeper into the natural landscape.

Feel the warmth of the sun on your skin or the cool breeze brushing against your face. Smell the fragrances of the natural surroundings – the earthy scent of soil, the sweetness of flowers, or the saltiness of the sea. Engage all your senses to fully immerse yourself in the beauty of nature.

Imagine a gentle stream or a serene lake within your mind. Picture yourself sitting by the water's edge. Dip your fingers into the water and feel its cool, soothing touch. As you connect with the water, visualise any stress or negativity washing away.

Allow the water to cleanse your mind and spirit, leaving you refreshed and revitalised. Sense the fluidity of emotions, mirroring the graceful movement of the water. Embrace the calmness and clarity that water brings.

As you gently bring your awareness back to the present moment, carry the serenity and connection with nature with you. Take a moment to express gratitude for the grounding experience and the beauty of the natural world.

When you're ready, slowly open your eyes, feeling rejuvenated and deeply connected to the harmony of nature. Carry this sense of peace with you as you go about your day, knowing that you can return to this place of tranquillity whenever needed.

Breath of Nature (8-12 Minutes)

Find a quiet space where you can sit or lie down comfortably. Close your eyes and take a few slow, deep breaths, inhaling the freshness of the air and exhaling any tension or stress. As you breathe, allow yourself to become present in this moment.

Inhale deeply, feeling the air fill your lungs with vitality. Picture yourself in an open field, surrounded by the natural world. With each breath, sense the energy of the earth entering your body. As you exhale, release any worries or distractions.

Visualise roots extending from the soles of your feet, anchoring you into the earth. Imagine these roots absorbing the nourishing energy of the soil. Feel a profound connection as the energy flows through your roots, grounding you in the present moment.

Take a moment to express gratitude for the Earth's support. Sense the stability and strength it provides, allowing you to stand tall like a resilient tree.

Slowly bring your awareness to each of your senses. Listen to the sounds of nature around you – the rustling leaves, the chirping birds, or the gentle flow of a stream. Feel the textures beneath you, whether it's soft grass, cool stone, or warm sand.

Inhale deeply, taking in the scents that surround you – the fragrance of flowers, the earthiness of the soil, or the freshness of the breeze. Engage with the natural world through your senses, immersing yourself in its beauty.

Envision a serene river gently flowing in front of you. Watch the water's rhythmic movement, symbolising the flow of life. As you observe, release any thoughts or concerns into the river, allowing them to be carried away.

Sit by the riverbank, feeling the coolness of the water. Sense the peace that comes with letting go and allow the river to cleanse your mind, leaving you with a renewed sense of clarity.

Picture a grand mountain standing tall against the sky. Visualise yourself at the mountain's base, feeling the solid rock beneath your hands. As you connect with the mountain's stability, absorb its strength and resilience.

Imagine yourself ascending the mountain, overcoming challenges with each step. Reach the summit and experience a profound sense of accomplishment and peace. Feel the expansiveness of the mountain's energy merging with your own.

Gently bring your awareness back to the present moment, carrying the tranquillity and connection with nature with you. Express gratitude for this journey of elemental serenity.

When you're ready, open your eyes slowly, feeling rejuvenated and deeply connected to the natural world. Carry this sense of peace and harmony with you, knowing that you can return to this place of serenity whenever you need to reconnect with nature.

Deep Nature Connection (15 Minutes)

Find a quiet and comfortable space. Sit or lie down, gently close your eyes, and take a moment to let go of the outside world. Inhale deeply, feeling the air fill your lungs with a sense of calm, and exhale, releasing any tension or distractions.

Visualise yourself in a lush, ancient forest. Picture the towering trees around you. Imagine roots extending from the soles of your feet, weaving into the rich soil beneath. Feel the strength and stability as you become one with the Earth.

Acknowledge the supportive energy of the forest, and with each breath, draw in the grounding force that surrounds you.

Shift your focus upward. Picture a vast, clear sky above the forest. With each inhale, absorb the expansive energy of the sky. Feel it filling your being with a sense of openness and limitless potential.

As you exhale, release any self-imposed limitations or doubts. Embrace the vastness of the sky within you.

Picture a gentle river winding through the forest. Imagine yourself sitting by the riverbank. As you gaze at the flowing water, recognise it as a reflection of the constant flow of life.

Allow your thoughts to drift away with the river. Feel the serenity that comes with letting go of the need to control every aspect of your life.

Become aware of the gentle breeze weaving through the trees. Imagine it carrying with it the whispers of nature. As you inhale, feel the cool, refreshing air filling your lungs.

Sense the harmony in the breeze, connecting you with the essence of the natural world. Exhale, releasing any remnants of stress.

Picture sunlight filtering through the leaves, creating patterns of dappled light on the forest floor. As you bask in this sunlight, visualise it illuminating your mind.

Inhale the clarity and warmth of the sunlight, allowing it to dissolve any mental fog or uncertainty. Exhale, releasing confusion and embracing mental clarity.

Begin walking along a forest path in your mind. Notice the textures under your feet, the sounds of leaves crunching, and the varied scents around you. Embrace the sensory richness of the forest.

With each step, feel a deeper connection to the earth. Allow the forest to guide you, trusting in the journey.

Imagine encountering an animal guide on your path. It could be a wise owl, a playful deer, or any creature that appears. Feel a sense of kinship with this guide, acknowledging the wisdom it imparts.

Allow the guide to lead you to a place of significance within the forest, deepening your connection to nature.

Arrive at a sacred clearing within the forest. Picture a serene space with a soft, mossy floor. Sit or lie down in this clearing, feeling the energy of the natural surroundings enveloping you.

Take a moment to appreciate the sacredness of this space, knowing it is a reflection of the sanctity within you.

Acknowledge the elements around you – earth, air, water, and fire. Feel the balance and integration of these elements within yourself. As you breathe, envision each element contributing to your overall wellbeing.

Embrace the grounding solidity of earth, the clarity of air, the flowing adaptability of water, and the transformative warmth of fire.

Allow the healing energy of the forest to permeate your being. Visualise the energy as a vibrant green light, entering your body with each breath. Feel it nourishing and rejuvenating every cell.

Inhale the vitality of the forest, and with each exhale, release any lingering tension or discomfort.

Tune into the changing seasons within the forest. Picture the vibrant colours of autumn leaves, the blossoming flowers of spring, the warmth of summer, and the tranquillity of winter.

Recognise the cyclical nature of life, with each season bringing its unique gifts and lessons.

Picture a majestic waterfall in the heart of the forest. Hear the powerful rush of water as it cascades down, cleansing everything in its path. Imagine standing under the waterfall, feeling its purifying energy.

Allow the waterfall to wash away any residual stress or negativity, leaving you refreshed and renewed.

As you gently bring your awareness back to the present moment, carry the serene energy and connection with nature with you. Express gratitude for the journey you've experienced.

When you're ready, slowly open your eyes, feeling revitalised and deeply connected to the symphony of nature's embrace. Carry this sense of peace with you, knowing that you can revisit this inner sanctuary of nature whenever you need.

15. PEACE

In the expansive realm of mindfulness, the pursuit of peace stands as a noble journey, inviting individuals to traverse the inner landscapes of tranquillity and harmony. Rooted in ancient contemplative traditions and embraced by modern mindfulness practices, the cultivation of peace involves a deliberate and present awareness that transcends the cacophony of daily life. Research in psychology and neuroscience underscores the profound impact of mindfulness on promoting a peaceful state of being. Studies suggest that regular engagement in mindfulness practices, such as meditation and mindful breathing, can lead to reduced stress levels, enhanced emotional regulation, and an overall sense of calmness. By anchoring themselves in the present moment, individuals create a sanctuary of peace that ripples through their thoughts, emotions, and interactions. As we navigate the landscapes of mindfulness, the pursuit of peace becomes a transformative odyssey, inviting individuals to embrace the serenity that dwells within and, in turn, contribute to a more peaceful and interconnected world.

A Peaceful Moment (3-5 minutes)

Find a quiet and comfortable space where you won't be disturbed. Sit or lie down in a relaxed position. Close your eyes and take a few deep breaths to settle into the present moment.

Begin by bringing your attention to your breath. Inhale deeply through your nose, feeling the breath fill your lungs, and exhale slowly through your mouth, releasing any tension. Take a few more breaths like this, allowing each inhale to bring calm and each exhale to release stress.

Now, imagine a gentle stream of light above your head, a soft and peaceful energy. With each breath, visualise this soothing light descending down into the crown of your head. Feel it as it moves through your body, bringing tranquillity to every muscle, every cell.

As the light continues to flow down, imagine it reaching your shoulders, releasing any tension or tightness. Let it cascade down your arms, all the way to your fingertips, bringing a sense of ease and serenity.

Allow the light to travel down your spine, soothing each vertebra. Feel it spreading through your chest, calming your heart and bringing a deep sense of peace to your entire being.

As the light reaches your abdomen, imagine it gently massaging any areas of discomfort or stress. Let it flow down to your hips, thighs, and knees, melting away any tension as it goes.

Now, visualise the light moving down your legs, all the way to your toes. Feel a warm and tranquil energy grounding you to the present moment. Your entire body is now enveloped in a cocoon of peace.

Take a moment to connect with this inner peace. Notice how your body feels, how your breath has become steady, and how your mind has become still. Embrace this sense of calmness, allowing it to permeate every aspect of your being.

Now, shift your focus to your heart centre. Imagine a radiant light glowing within your chest, the source of pure love and compassion. With each breath, let this light expand, filling your entire body and radiating out into the space around you.

Extend this loving light beyond yourself, sending it to those around you, your loved ones, and even to those with whom you may have challenges. Imagine a web of connection, a network of peace and understanding.

As you bask in this peaceful energy, affirm to yourself:

"I am peace. I am love."

"I am connected to the tranquillity within and around me."

Take a few more deep breaths, gradually bringing your awareness back to the present moment. When you feel ready, gently open your eyes.

Carry this sense of peace with you throughout your day, knowing that you can return to this guided meditation whenever you need to reconnect with the calm within.

Finding Inner Peace (8-12 Minutes)

Find a comfortable and quiet space to sit or lie down. Close your eyes and take a few deep breaths to centre yourself. Let go of any tension as you settle into a relaxed posture.

Begin by focusing on your breath. Inhale deeply through your nose, allowing your lungs to fill with air, and exhale slowly through your mouth, releasing any stress or tension. Continue to breathe naturally, feeling the rhythm of your breath as it connects you to the present moment.

Shift your attention to your body. With each breath, imagine a wave of relaxation starting from the top of your head. Feel it gently cascading down, bringing a sense of calm to your forehead, eyes, and jaw. Release any tension in your neck and shoulders, letting the soothing wave flow down your arms to your fingertips.

As the wave moves down your spine, sense the muscles relaxing, allowing any stress to dissolve. Let it continue down to your chest, abdomen, and hips, softening and releasing any tightness. Feel the wave of relaxation moving through your legs, all the way down to your toes.

Picture yourself in a tranquil natural setting. It could be a serene forest, a peaceful meadow, or a quiet beach. Visualise the beauty of nature surrounding you – gentle breezes, the rustling of leaves, or the sound of waves. Feel a deep connection to the earth beneath you.

Imagine absorbing the peaceful energy of nature. As you breathe in, visualise the clean and refreshing air filling your lungs. With each exhale, release any remaining tension and feel a sense of grounding.

Envision a serene and safe inner sanctuary. It could be a cozy room, a peaceful garden, or any place that brings you comfort. Explore the details of this sanctuary – colours, textures, and scents. This is your personal space of tranquillity.

Take a moment to sit or lie down in your inner sanctuary, feeling completely at ease. Allow the sense of peace in this space to wash over you, enveloping you in a warm and soothing embrace.

Shift your focus to your heart centre. Imagine a soft, glowing light emanating from this area. With each breath, feel this light expanding, radiating warmth and compassion.

Extend this loving light beyond yourself, sending it to loved ones, friends, and even those with whom you may have challenges. Visualise the light creating connections, fostering understanding, and promoting peace in the hearts of those around you.

As you bask in this peaceful energy, silently repeat affirmations to yourself:

"I am peace. I am love."

"I am connected to the tranquillity within and around me."

Express gratitude for this moment of inner calm and the ability to carry this peace with you into the world.

Gently bring your awareness back to your breath. Take a few deep breaths, gradually becoming aware of your surroundings. When you feel ready, open your eyes with a renewed sense of peace.

Carry this tranquil energy with you throughout your day, and know that you can return to this guided meditation whenever you need to reconnect with the serenity within.

A Journey to Deep Peace (15 Minutes)

Find a quiet and comfortable space where you can sit or lie down. Close your eyes and take a moment to settle into a relaxed position. Allow your awareness to shift from the external world to your internal experience.

Start by taking a few deep breaths, inhaling slowly through your nose and exhaling through your mouth. As you breathe, let go of any tension or stress. Imagine you are releasing any thoughts or concerns with each exhale.

Bring your attention to your body. Scan through your body from head to toe, noticing any areas of tension or discomfort. As you identify these areas, visualise a warm and gentle light surrounding them. With each breath, allow this light to soften and release any tightness or discomfort. Feel the warmth spreading through your body, bringing a deep sense of relaxation.

Shift your focus to your breath. Notice the natural rhythm of your breathing. Feel the coolness as you inhale and the warmth as you exhale. Allow your breath to guide you into a state of present awareness. If your mind begins to wander, gently bring it back to the sensation of breathing.

Imagine yourself sitting in the centre of a vast, open space. This space represents your mind, clear and expansive. As thoughts arise, visualise them as clouds passing through the open sky of your mind. Acknowledge each thought without judgment and let it drift away, leaving the sky clear and serene.

Bring attention to the sounds around you. Notice the distant sounds and those close by. Instead of judging or labelling the sounds, observe them with a sense of curiosity. Allow the sounds to come and go, like ripples in a pond, without holding onto them. Let the act of listening anchor you to the present moment.

Shift your focus to cultivating feelings of love and kindness. Imagine a warm and compassionate light radiating from your heart. Begin by directing this light towards yourself, wishing for your own wellbeing and peace. Then, extend these feelings of love and kindness to others, envisioning friends, family, and even acquaintances, surrounded by the same warm light.

Reflect on the things you are grateful for in this moment. Visualise these aspects of your life, feeling a sense of appreciation and contentment. Picture a serene landscape that represents peace to you – whether it's a tranquil forest, a calm lake, or a quiet mountaintop.

Gently bring your awareness back to your breath. Take a few deep breaths, feeling the rise and fall of your chest. Gradually become aware of your physical surroundings. When you feel ready, slowly open your eyes.

Carry the sense of peace and relaxation with you into the rest of your day, knowing that you can return to this guided meditation whenever you seek a moment of calm reflection and inner harmony.

16. POSITIVE EMOTIONS

In the vast landscape of mindfulness, a radiant meadow is adorned with the blossoms of positive emotions, a terrain explored and nurtured through contemplative practices. Positive emotions, integral to the fabric of wellbeing, play a pivotal role in the cultivation of mindfulness. Delving into moments of joy, gratitude, and compassion, individuals embark on a journey that transcends mere awareness, extending into the realm of profound emotional flourishing. Research in the field of psychology and neuroscience underscores the transformative power of mindfulness in fostering positive emotions. Studies reveal that regular mindfulness practices can contribute to an amplification of positive affect, a heightened sense of life satisfaction, and increased emotional resilience. By deliberately directing attention to the present moment without judgment, individuals can unearth a reservoir of positive emotions that not only enrich their inner lives but also radiate outward, influencing interpersonal connections and the overall quality of life. As we explore the intersection of mindfulness and positive emotions, a vibrant tapestry unfolds, inviting individuals to embrace the full spectrum of their emotional experiences with open hearts and mindful awareness.

Radiant Positivity (3-5 minutes)

Find a quiet and comfortable place to sit or lie down. Close your eyes and take a few deep breaths to relax your body and mind.

Imagine a warm, golden light surrounding you. This light represents positivity and joy. Picture it gently enveloping your body, creating a protective and uplifting aura.

Inhale deeply through your nose, counting to four, and exhale slowly through your mouth, counting to six. With each breath, imagine the golden light expanding within you, filling every cell with positive energy.

Bring your attention to your toes. Feel the warmth and positivity spreading from your toes to the top of your head, like a wave of soothing energy. Take your time and enjoy the sensation.

Visualise a beautiful garden. As you explore, notice the vibrant colours, the soothing sounds of nature, and the pleasant fragrances. With each step, express gratitude for something in your life – big or small. Feel the warmth of appreciation radiating from your heart.

Repeat to yourself:

"I am filled with love and joy."

"I attract positivity into my life."

"I am grateful for the abundance that surrounds me."

Imagine yourself in a peaceful natural setting, perhaps a serene forest or a tranquil beach. Feel the connection with nature, absorbing its calmness and positive energy. Visualise the sun shining above, filling you with warmth and radiance.

Envision yourself surrounded by loved ones, friends, and acquaintances. See them smiling and happy. Imagine sending waves of positive energy towards them, wishing them well. Feel the interconnectedness of your positive emotions with those around you.

Gradually bring your awareness back to the room. Wiggle your fingers and toes. When you're ready, open your eyes.

Before concluding, affirm to yourself:

"I carry this positivity with me throughout the day."

"I am a beacon of joy and gratitude."

Take a moment to appreciate the positive feelings you've cultivated during this meditation. Carry this sense of wellbeing with you as you go about your day.

Inner Bliss (8-12 Minutes)

Find a quiet, comfortable space and sit in a relaxed position. Close your eyes and take a few deep breaths to centre yourself. Allow the outside world to fade away as you turn your attention inward.

Imagine roots extending from your body into the earth below. Feel a sense of grounding as these roots anchor you to the present moment. With each breath, draw up the nourishing energy from the earth into your being.

Inhale deeply through your nose, drawing in positive energy, and exhale through your mouth, releasing any tension or negativity. With each breath, envision a bright light expanding within you, rejuvenating your mind, body, and spirit.

Visualise a spectrum of colours surrounding you. Each colour represents a different positive emotion – love, joy, gratitude, peace, and contentment. Picture these colours blending and swirling, creating a vibrant and harmonious aura around you.

Place your hands over your heart and focus on the warmth emanating from this area. Bring to mind three things you're grateful for. As you reflect on each one, let the feeling of gratitude expand, filling your entire being with a sense of appreciation.

Envision a gentle river flowing within you, representing positivity and optimism. Imagine yourself floating on this river, allowing its current to carry you towards a brighter and more uplifting state of mind.

Surround yourself with a circle of positivity. Repeat the following affirmations:

"I am deserving of happiness."

"I attract positivity into my life effortlessly."

"Every breath I take fills me with joy and peace."

Picture yourself in a serene sanctuary, a place that represents tranquillity and happiness. It could be a meadow, a beach, or a cosy room. Feel the safety and comfort of this space, allowing it to amplify your positive emotions.

Imagine a radiant sun within your chest, glowing with warmth and light. As you breathe, feel this sun expanding, spreading its positive energy throughout your entire body. Sense its rays reaching every corner of your being, dissolving any lingering negativity.

Extend your positive energy beyond yourself. Envision beams of light emanating from your heart and reaching out to the people around you, your community, and the world. Feel a connection as you contribute to the collective wellbeing.

Slowly become aware of your surroundings. Wiggle your fingers and toes. Take a moment to appreciate the positivity you've cultivated. When you're ready, gently open your eyes.

Before concluding, express gratitude for the positive emotions you've generated. Carry this sense of inner bliss with you as you navigate the rest of your day.

Joyful Smiles (15 Minutes)

Find a comfortable position, sitting with a straight back. Close your eyes gently and take a few deep breaths. Release any tension as you exhale, letting go of the cares of the day.

Inhale slowly through your nose, counting to four, and exhale through your mouth, counting to six. Feel each breath calming your body and mind. As you exhale, visualise any stress or negativity leaving your body.

Bring your awareness to different parts of your body, starting with your toes. Notice any tension, and with each exhale, imagine that tension melting away. Gradually work your way up to the top of your head, releasing any knots or tightness.

Picture a warm, gentle light forming at the centre of your chest. As you breathe, visualise this light expanding, radiating positivity. Imagine the light taking the form of a soothing smile, filling your entire being with a sense of joy and warmth.

Think of three things you're grateful for. With each one, allow a genuine smile to form on your face. Feel the gratitude filling your heart and radiating through your entire being. Smile as you acknowledge the positive aspects of your life.

Bring your attention to your body. Begin to smile softly at each part of your body. From your toes to the top of your head, express appreciation for the functions and sensations each part provides. Feel a sense of gratitude for the vessel that carries you through life.

Inhale slowly through your nose, imagining that you are breathing in a bright, golden light. As you exhale through your mouth, picture that light spreading through your body, infusing every cell with positivity. Smile with each breath, allowing the joy to grow.

Envision a place that makes you incredibly happy. It could be a beach, a mountain, or a cosy room. Imagine yourself there, surrounded by the elements that bring you joy. Feel the happiness and let it manifest as a smile on your face.

Picture waves of laughter washing over you. Visualise the sound of laughter like gentle waves, reaching every part of your being. Let the infectious joy fill you, and allow a spontaneous smile or even a giggle to emerge.

Visualise the faces of people you love and care about. Picture them smiling back at you. Feel the warmth and connection as their smiles mirror your own. Sense the positive energy flowing between you and them.

Consider challenges you've faced. Smile as you acknowledge the strength and resilience within you. Recognise that every challenge is an opportunity for growth and learning, and appreciate the positive aspects that have emerged from difficult situations.

Project your thoughts to the future with a smile. Picture yourself achieving your goals and living a fulfilling life. Embrace the positive possibilities that lie ahead, and let a genuine smile light up your face.

Visualise yourself surrounded by a radiant light. With each breath, feel this light expanding beyond your body, creating a bubble of positivity around you. Smile as you become a beacon of joy and love.

Take a moment to smile at yourself. Imagine looking into a mirror and seeing the joy and positivity reflected back at you. Smile even brighter as you acknowledge the beauty of your authentic, happy self.

Slowly bring your awareness back to the present. Take a deep breath, and as you exhale, smile at the gratitude you feel for this moment of peace and positivity. When you're ready, gently open your eyes, bringing the warmth of your smiles into the world around you.

17. SAVOURING

In the tapestry of mindfulness, the art of savouring emerges as a vibrant thread, weaving through the moments of our lives with a deliberate and appreciative awareness. Rooted in the present moment, savouring involves a mindful engagement with the richness of our experiences, inviting us to fully taste the flavours of joy, beauty, and contentment that life offers. Research in psychology and contemplative science suggests that incorporating savouring practices into our daily routines can lead to profound shifts in wellbeing. Studies indicate that individuals who cultivate the ability to savour moments experience increased positive emotions, enhanced life satisfaction, and a deeper sense of gratitude. By intentionally slowing down, paying attention, and relishing the nuances of positive experiences, individuals can create a reservoir of positive memories and a heightened appreciation for the simple pleasures of life. As we journey through the realms of mindfulness, the practice of savouring becomes a mindful celebration, encouraging individuals to embrace the fullness of their experiences and savour the sweetness of each passing moment.

Savouring Serenity (3-5 minutes)

Before we begin, I invite you to prepare a cup of tea or coffee, or perhaps grab a small snack. Having a cup of tea or a snack nearby will enhance your experience during this meditation, allowing you to fully engage your senses. When you're ready, join me in the practice of savouring the present moment.

Find a comfortable and quiet space where you won't be disturbed. Sit or lie down in a relaxed position, with your spine straight and your hands resting comfortably. Close your eyes, take a deep breath in, and exhale slowly. Let go of any tension in your body.

Start by bringing your awareness to your breath. Inhale deeply through your nose, allowing the breath to fill your lungs, and exhale slowly through your mouth. Repeat this for a few breaths, focusing on the sensation of the breath entering and leaving your body. Let each breath anchor you to the present moment.

Now, shift your attention to different parts of your body, starting from your toes and gradually moving up to the top of your head. Notice any sensations or tension. As you breathe out, release any tension you may be holding in each part of your body. Feel a sense of relaxation spreading through you with each breath.

Take a moment to become aware of your surroundings. Notice any sounds, smells, or sensations around you. Feel the support of the surface beneath you. Acknowledge the present moment without judgment.

Focus your attention on your senses. Begin with the sense of touch – feel the warmth or coolness of the air on your skin. Notice any textures beneath your hands. Move on to the sense of hearing – listen to the sounds around you, both near and far. Appreciate the symphony of life.

If you have a cup of tea, coffee, or a small snack nearby, take a moment to savour it. Pay attention to the taste and texture. Notice the aroma. Allow each sip or bite to be an opportunity to fully engage your senses. If you don't have anything to taste, imagine the sensations of your favourite food.

Reflect on the simple pleasures of this moment. Express gratitude for the ability to experience these sensations. Acknowledge the beauty in the ordinary.

As you slowly bring your awareness back to the room, take a few deep breaths. Wiggle your fingers and toes, gradually awakening your body. When you're ready, open your eyes.

Remember, the practice of savouring is about fully experiencing and appreciating the richness of each moment. Carry this mindful awareness with you as you continue with your day.

Savouring the Present (8-12 Minutes)

Before we embark on this mindful journey, I invite you to prepare a snack or a drink. Find something you enjoy – a cup of tea, coffee, or a small snack. Having these items nearby will enhance your experience during this meditation, allowing you to fully engage your senses. When you're ready, join me in the practice of savouring the present moment.

Begin by finding a quiet and comfortable space. Sit or lie down in a relaxed position, allowing your body to settle into a state of ease. Take a moment to let go of the demands of the day and be fully present in this space.

Close your eyes and turn your attention inward. Start by taking a deep breath in, feeling the air fill your lungs, and exhale slowly, releasing any tension or stress. Repeat this a few times, allowing each breath to deepen your sense of relaxation.

Bring your awareness to the natural rhythm of your breath. Notice the sensation as you inhale and exhale. Feel the gentle rise and fall of your chest and abdomen. Allow your breath to be your anchor to the present moment.

your attention to your body. Starting from your toes, slowly scan through each part, bringing awareness to any areas of tension or relaxation. As you breathe out, release any tightness, allowing a wave of calm to wash over you.

Gradually open your senses to the world around you. Listen to the sounds in your environment, whether it's the rustling of leaves, distant sounds, or the quiet hum of your surroundings. Take a moment to appreciate the richness of the auditory tapestry.

Shift your awareness to the sense of touch. Feel the points of contact between your body and the surface beneath you. Notice the temperature of the air on your skin and any sensations arising. Allow yourself to fully feel the present moment through the sense of touch.

With your eyes still closed, envision a peaceful scene. It could be a serene landscape, a comforting place, or simply a space filled with tranquillity. Explore the vividness of this mental image, appreciating the details and colours that come to mind.

Bring your attention to any scents in the air. Whether it's the aroma of nature, a comforting fragrance, or the subtle scent of your surroundings, take a moment to inhale deeply and appreciate the olfactory experience.

If you have a cup of tea, coffee, or a small snack nearby, take a moment to savour it. Pay attention to the taste, texture, and temperature. Allow each sip or bite to be a mindful experience, fully engaging your senses in the act of nourishment.

Reflect on the aspects of this present moment that bring you joy and gratitude. It could be the simple pleasures, the people in your life, or the opportunities that surround you. Express appreciation for the richness of your experiences.

As you continue to breathe deeply, bring your attention back to the present moment. Embrace the feeling of being fully alive and aware. Each breath is an opportunity to immerse yourself in the beauty of now.

Gently bring your awareness back to the room. Wiggle your fingers and toes, and when you're ready, open your eyes. Take a moment to acknowledge the serenity you've cultivated and carry this sense of presence with you as you step back into your day.

Remember, the art of savouring is about embracing each moment with openness and appreciation. May the mindfulness you've cultivated stay with you, creating a lasting sense of peace.

Embracing the Fullness of Now (15 Minutes)

Before we dive into this mindful exploration, let's take a moment to prepare. Grab a comforting drink or a delightful snack – something that brings you joy. Having these simple pleasures within reach will add a layer of richness to our meditation. So, when you're ready, join me in savouring the fullness of the present moment.

Find a quiet and comfortable space where you can sit or lie down. Ensure that you won't be disturbed during this time. Take a moment to settle into a comfortable position, allowing your body to relax and your mind to let go of any preoccupations.

Close your eyes and begin with a few deep breaths. Inhale deeply through your nose, hold for a moment, and exhale slowly through your mouth. Feel the rise and fall of your chest and abdomen. Let each breath draw you into the present moment.

Shift your focus to your physical body. Notice any sensations, warmth, or coolness. Scan through each part of your body, from the tips of your toes to the top of your head. If you encounter any tension, breathe into those areas and let the tension dissolve with each exhale.

Feel the connection between your body and the surface beneath you. Whether you're sitting or lying down, sense the support that holds you. Allow yourself to be grounded in this moment, appreciating the stability and security it provides.

Gradually open your eyes, taking in the visual landscape around you. Notice the colours, shapes, and textures in your immediate environment. Embrace the richness of what you see without needing to label or analyse.

Close your eyes once again and shift your attention to the sounds around you. Listen to the symphony of life – distant sounds, nature, or even the subtle hum of your own surroundings. Let the sounds wash over you, embracing each one without judgment.

Return to your breath, focusing on the sensation of each inhale and exhale. Notice the natural rhythm and flow. If your mind starts to wander, gently guide it back to the breath. Use this anchor to bring yourself back to the present.

Bring awareness to the sensations of touch. Feel the fabric of your clothing against your skin, the temperature of the air, and any textures your hands may encounter. Allow yourself to be fully present through the sense of touch.

If you feel comfortable, gently move your body. Stretch your limbs, roll your shoulders, or wiggle your fingers and toes. Acknowledge the gift of movement and the vitality it brings to your experience.

Choose an object in your immediate surroundings. Study it with curiosity, exploring its details. Notice the play of light, shadows, and colours. Allow this focused observation to deepen your connection to the present.

If you have a snack or a cup of tea, take a moment to savour it mindfully. Pay attention to the taste, texture, and aroma. Let each bite or sip be a celebration of the senses, fully engaging with the experience.

Imagine yourself in a natural setting – a forest, a beach, or a meadow. Visualise the beauty of nature around you. Feel the connection with the earth, the sky, and the elements. Allow the sense of nature's presence to infuse you with calmness.

Reflect on a recent moment that brought you joy or contentment. It could be a small, ordinary moment that often goes unnoticed. Dive into the details of that experience and rekindle the positive emotions associated with it.

Take a mental journey through your life, recalling moments and experiences for which you are grateful. Express gratitude for the people, opportunities, and simple pleasures that have enriched your journey. Allow gratitude to fill your heart.

Extend your awareness to the people in your life. Send thoughts of love, kindness, and wellbeing to those around you. Visualise a circle of warmth and positive energy expanding from your heart to encompass your loved ones.

As you bring this meditation to a close, take a few moments to reflect on the sensations and emotions you've experienced. Gradually transition back to your everyday awareness, knowing that you can carry this mindful presence with you into the rest of your day.

Open your eyes when you're ready, feeling rejuvenated and deeply connected to the fullness of the present moment. May the practice of savouring continue to enrich your life.

18. SLEEP

In the realm of mindfulness, the significance of sleep emerges as a foundational pillar supporting overall wellbeing and mental health. Mindful sleep practices invite individuals to approach bedtime with a deliberate and present awareness, recognising the profound impact that quality sleep has on physical and mental rejuvenation. Research in the fields of sleep science and mindfulness indicates that incorporating mindful techniques into bedtime routines can lead to improved sleep quality and overall sleep hygiene. Mindfulness-based interventions, such as mindful breathing and body scan practices, have been shown to reduce insomnia symptoms and contribute to a more restful night's sleep. By cultivating a mindful approach to sleep, individuals may find themselves better equipped to navigate the challenges of daily life, experiencing heightened alertness, emotional resilience, and improved cognitive function. As we explore the dimensions of mindfulness, the practice of mindful sleep becomes a nurturing journey, inviting individuals to create a sanctuary for rest and rejuvenation, ultimately contributing to a more vibrant and balanced life.

Tranquil Slumber (3-5 minutes)

Begin by finding a comfortable position, lying down in your bed with your arms resting gently by your sides. Take a moment to settle into the softness of your mattress and feel the weight of your body sinking into a state of relaxation.

Close your eyes and turn your attention to your breath. Inhale deeply through your nose, allowing your lungs to fill with soothing air. Feel your chest and abdomen rise as you breathe in. Exhale slowly through your mouth, releasing any tension or stress with each breath. Continue this rhythmic breathing, allowing each inhale and exhale to wash over you like gentle waves.

As you continue to breathe deeply, bring your awareness to different parts of your body, starting from your toes and working your way up. With each breath, imagine a warm, soft light enveloping that part of your body, melting away any tension or tightness. Picture the light moving slowly upward, bringing tranquillity to each area it touches. Allow this gentle warmth to relax your feet, ankles, calves, and so on, until your entire body is embraced by a comforting sense of calm.

Imagine yourself in a serene place, perhaps a peaceful meadow, a tranquil beach, or a quiet forest. Picture the details of this place – the colours, the sounds, the gentle breeze. As you immerse yourself in this mental sanctuary, let go of any thoughts that may be lingering from the day. Imagine placing each thought on a gentle cloud, watching it float away into the distance.

Shift your focus to gratitude. Bring to mind three things you are grateful for today. These can be simple pleasures or moments of joy. As you reflect on these aspects of your life, feel a sense of warmth and appreciation filling your heart.

Now, as you prepare to drift into a restful sleep, repeat these positive affirmations to yourself:

"I am safe and secure."

"I release the events of the day."

"I embrace the tranquillity of the night".

Continue to breathe deeply, embracing the sense of calm and relaxation that surrounds you. Allow yourself to surrender to the peaceful embrace of sleep, knowing that you are in a safe and nurturing space.

As you conclude this meditation, carry this serene energy into your dreams, letting go of the day and welcoming the healing power of a restful night's sleep. Sweet dreams.

Embracing Serenity (8-12 Minutes)

Begin by finding a comfortable position in your bed. Allow your body to settle into the softness beneath you. Close your eyes gently, and take a moment to acknowledge the stillness around you.

Inhale deeply through your nose, drawing in the essence of calmness. Feel the soothing air fill your lungs, expanding your chest and abdomen. Exhale slowly through your mouth, releasing any tension or worry. With each breath, imagine a gentle breeze carrying away the burdens of the day, leaving you in a state of tranquillity.

Visualise yourself floating on a serene lake, bathed in the soft glow of moonlight. Picture the water beneath you as a liquid cradle, gently rocking you back and forth. Feel the coolness of the water soothing your body, and sense the serenity of the moonlight embracing you in a cocoon of tranquillity.

Bring awareness to your body, starting with your toes. Feel the weight of each toe, acknowledging the pull of gravity. Gradually move your attention upward, allowing each part of your body to surrender to the gentle force holding you to the earth. Experience a profound sense of release as you let go, sinking into the mattress with each passing moment.

Envision a shower of gentle starlight raining down from above. As the starlight touches your body, imagine it cleansing away any residual stress or tension. Picture each starlight droplet dissolving any negative energy, leaving only a radiant glow of tranquillity in its wake.

Listen to the symphony of the night. Hear the soothing sounds of crickets, the distant rustling of leaves, and the rhythmic beat of your own heart. Allow these natural melodies to guide you deeper into a state of relaxation, creating a harmonious background for your journey into the realm of sleep.

Reflect on the positive moments of your day. Consider three things you're grateful for, allowing each grateful thought to wrap you in a warm embrace. Let gratitude be the lullaby that carries you into a restful slumber.

As you feel the gentle pull of sleep, imagine a vivid and pleasant dream awaiting you. Picture yourself in a place of joy and serenity. Allow the details of this dream to unfold, embracing the sense of wonder and happiness it brings.

Repeat to yourself:

"I am deserving of a peaceful sleep."

"I surrender to the healing power of rest."

"Tomorrow is a new day filled with possibilities."

Let these affirmations guide you into a state of profound relaxation.

As you continue to breathe deeply, feel yourself drifting further into the realm of dreams. Trust in the night to cradle you in its comforting embrace, allowing you to surrender to the gentle currents of sleep.

Express gratitude for the gift of this moment. Thank yourself for the effort you've put into this meditation. With a heart full of gratitude and a mind ready to rest, bid yourself a good night, knowing that sleep will welcome you warmly.

Allow yourself to continue drifting into a deep and restful sleep, carried by the soothing energy of serenity's embrace. Sweet dreams.

Morpheus' Embrace (15 Minutes)

Begin by settling into a comfortable position in your bed. Close your eyes gently and take a moment to release the tension from your body. As you embark on this journey, open your mind to the realm of dreams and the embrace of Morpheus, the god of dreams.

Inhale deeply through your nose, drawing in the essence of tranquillity. Feel the breath fill your lungs, expanding your chest and abdomen. As you exhale, release any lingering thoughts or worries. With each breath, invite a sense of surrender, allowing the weight of the day to dissolve.

Imagine standing at the threshold of a peaceful garden, Morpheus' realm. Picture a beautiful gate before you, adorned with vines and flowers. As you step through, feel a wave of calm wash over you. This is the gateway to restful dreams.

Listen to the celestial symphony that Morpheus orchestrates. Imagine the gentle hum of cosmic melodies, a harmonious blend of the moon's whispers, stars twinkling, and the soothing hum of your own heartbeat. Let these ethereal sounds guide you into a state of deep relaxation.

Envision yourself lying on a soft cloud, gently floating through Morpheus' dream garden. Feel the cloud cradle you, moulding to the contours of your body. Allow a sense of weightlessness to envelop you, freeing you from any remaining tension.

As you float, notice the colours around you. Morpheus' garden is painted in hues that inspire serenity and peace. Each colour has a calming effect, and you can feel their gentle touch as you drift through this dreamland.

Spot blossoms of gratitude growing around you. With each flower, reflect on something you're thankful for. As you do, watch the blossoms multiply, creating a garden of gratitude that surrounds you with positive energy.

Sense Morpheus' gentle presence as he whispers sweet lullabies to guide you into a restful sleep. Allow his soothing words to fill your mind, creating a tranquil sanctuary for your thoughts.

Feel yourself gently lifting from the cloud, entering the astral plane of dreams. Picture a tapestry of dreams unfolding before you. Each thread represents a possibility, a beautiful dream waiting to be explored.

Choose a thread that calls to you. Follow it through the tapestry, unveiling a vivid dream scenario. Engage your senses in this dream world – feel the textures, hear the sounds, and immerse yourself in the colours. Morpheus is your guide, leading you through a landscape of peaceful and enchanting dreams.

As you continue your journey, imagine a gentle shower of starlight cleansing your spirit. Let this celestial light wash away any residual stress or worries, leaving you pure and refreshed in Morpheus' embrace.

Whisper sleep affirmations to yourself:

"I welcome restful dreams."

"My mind is at ease."

"I trust in the healing power of sleep."

Feel these affirmations resonating within you, affirming your readiness for a peaceful night's sleep.

Arrive at a place of cosmic stillness. Feel the vastness of the dream universe around you, a tranquil space where time slows and worries dissipate. Rest in this cosmic stillness as you prepare to transition into a deeper state of slumber.

Imagine yourself soaring through the night sky, guided by Morpheus himself. Glide effortlessly among the stars, a celestial dance leading you towards a profound and restful sleep.

Feel Morpheus' presence beside you, offering a gentle blessing for restful dreams. Sense his energy enveloping you like a comforting embrace, ensuring a peaceful and rejuvenating night's sleep.

As you feel the call of sleep, allow yourself to drift gently into the dream realm. Trust that Morpheus will guide your journey, weaving a tapestry of dreams that bring you solace and joy. Surrender to the peaceful embrace of Morpheus as you float into the world of restful dreams.

May Morpheus' embrace accompany you through the night, and may your dreams be filled with tranquillity. Goodnight and sweet dreams.

19. STRESS RELEASE

In the fast-paced symphony of modern life, the quest for serenity and inner peace has become increasingly vital for navigating the complexities of stress and uncertainty. Within the realms of mindfulness, meditation practices specifically designed to release stress and cultivate a serene inner landscape offer a sanctuary for the weary soul. Grounded in ancient contemplative traditions, these meditative journeys guide individuals towards a profound state of tranquillity. Contemporary research in psychology and neuroscience has shed light on the transformative effects of such practices. Studies suggest that regular engagement in stress-release meditations is associated with a reduction in cortisol levels, the body's primary stress hormone, leading to a more relaxed physiological state. Additionally, individuals who incorporate these practices into their daily routines report improved emotional regulation, heightened clarity of thought, and an overall enhanced sense of wellbeing. As we explore the realms of mindfulness, the meditation for stress release emerges as a potent tool, inviting individuals to embark on an inner journey towards serenity and peace amidst life's tumultuous currents.

Serenity Within (3-5 minutes)

Begin by finding a comfortable and quiet place to sit or lie down. Close your eyes and take a few deep breaths, inhaling deeply through your nose and exhaling slowly through your mouth. Allow yourself to fully arrive in this present moment.

Start by bringing your awareness to your body. Feel the sensation of the ground beneath you, supporting you. Notice any areas of tension or discomfort. As you inhale, imagine breathing in relaxation, and as you exhale, release any tension you may be holding onto.

Focus your attention on your breath. Feel the gentle rise and fall of your chest or the sensation of the breath as it enters and leaves your nostrils. With each breath, imagine a wave of calm washing over you. Inhale peace, exhale tension.

Take a moment to tense and then release different muscle groups in your body. Start with your toes, tensing them for a few seconds and then releasing. Move up to your calves, thighs, and so on, working your way up to your head. As you release each muscle group, visualise the stress leaving your body.

Imagine yourself in a peaceful natural setting. It could be a beach, a forest, or a meadow. Picture the sights, sounds, and smells around you. Feel the warmth of the sun, the gentle rustle of leaves, or the soothing sound of waves. Allow the calming energy of nature to envelop you.

Bring your attention to the present moment without judgment. Notice any thoughts or feelings that arise, and let them pass without attaching to them. Imagine your thoughts as clouds passing by in the sky. Acknowledge them, but let them drift away, leaving your mind clear and calm.

Shift your focus to gratitude. Bring to mind three things you are thankful for in this moment. It could be simple things like the warmth of sunlight, the air you breathe, or the support you have in your life. Allow the positive feelings associated with gratitude to replace any lingering stress.

Take a few more deep breaths, gradually bringing your awareness back to the present. Wiggle your fingers and toes, and when you're ready, open your eyes. Carry this sense of calm and relaxation with you as you continue with your day.

Tranquil Harmony (8-12 Minutes)

Begin by finding a quiet and comfortable space. Sit or lie down in a relaxed position. Close your eyes gently and take a few moments to settle into the stillness around you. Allow the external world to fade away as you turn your attention inward.

Take a deep breath in, feeling the air fill your lungs, and exhale slowly, releasing any tension. With each breath, imagine roots extending from your body into the earth, grounding you to the present moment. Feel the support beneath you.

Shift your focus to your toes. Feel a warm, soothing energy spreading through them. Gradually move up through your feet, ankles, and legs, bringing a sense of relaxation to each body part. Release any tension you may encounter as you scan through your body.

Picture yourself in a tranquil garden. Notice the vibrant colours of the flowers, the gentle rustle of leaves, and the soft warmth of the sunlight. As you explore this serene space, imagine stress as dark clouds above you. With each breath, visualise these clouds dissipating, leaving only clear, calm skies.

Bring your attention back to your breath. Inhale positivity and exhale any remaining stress or worry. Feel the rhythm of your breath, steady and calming. Allow the breath to be an anchor for your mind, bringing you back to the present moment whenever needed.

Envision yourself on a peaceful beach. Picture the rhythmic ebb and flow of ocean waves. With each wave that washes ashore, imagine it carrying away any stress or tension from your body. Let the soothing sound of the waves create a sense of calm within you.

Repeat after me, positive affirmations related to release and relaxation:

"I release what I cannot control."

"I am at peace with this moment."

Allow these affirmations to resonate within you, fostering a mindset of letting go.

Acknowledge the interconnectedness of your mind and body.

Imagine a gentle flow of energy moving from your head to your toes, bringing a sense of harmony and balance. With each breath, visualise this healing energy, dissolving any remaining stress.

Take a moment to reflect on three things you are grateful for. Allow the warmth of gratitude to fill your heart and shift your focus from stress to appreciation. Feel a sense of abundance and joy in these moments of thankfulness.

Slowly bring your awareness back to the room. Wiggle your fingers and toes, becoming aware of your physical presence. When you're ready, open your eyes, carrying the tranquillity and peace you've cultivated into the rest of your day.

Finding Your Inner Peace (15 Minutes)

Find a quiet space where you can sit comfortably. Close your eyes and take a moment to disconnect from the outside world. Bring your attention to the gentle rise and fall of your breath.

Begin by focusing on your body. Take a deep breath and as you exhale, release any tension. Scan your body from head to toe, observing sensations without judgment. Notice areas of tightness, and with each breath, allow those areas to soften and relax.

Inhale deeply for a count of four, hold your breath for four, and exhale for a count of six. Feel the rhythm of your breath as it brings a sense of calm and balance to your body. Continue this pattern, letting each breath anchor you in the present moment.

Visualise a swirling ball of vibrant energy within your chest, representing stress. As you breathe out, imagine this ball expanding and releasing colourful streams of light in all directions. Each colour symbolises a different aspect of stress leaving your body.

Shift your attention to the sounds around you. Whether it's the distant hum of traffic, birdsong, or the rustling of leaves, simply observe without attaching any meaning. Allow these sounds to be a backdrop, grounding you in the present.

Picture yourself as a majestic mountain, rooted deeply into the earth. As storms of stress come and go, visualise the mountain standing strong and unshaken. Feel the stability and resilience within you.

Connect your breath with specific parts of your body. Inhale, directing your breath to your shoulders, and as you exhale, release tension from that area. Move through each part of your body, giving attention to where it's needed.

Imagine a gentle rain shower washing over you, cleansing away any remaining stress. Feel the droplets of water washing away worries, leaving you refreshed and revitalised. Embrace the sensation of renewal.

In your mind, create a gratitude journal. Reflect on three things you're grateful for today. Take a moment to savour the positive emotions associated with these experiences. Gratitude can be a powerful antidote to stress.

Bring awareness to your five senses. Notice the feeling of your breath, the scent in the air, the temperature on your skin, any tastes lingering in your mouth, and the sounds around you. Engaging your senses helps anchor you in the present moment.

Repeat self-compassionate affirmations:

"I am worthy of peace."

"I release what no longer serves me."

Let these affirmations resonate within you, fostering a sense of self-love and acceptance.

Envision yourself floating on a tranquil lake. Feel the gentle sway of the water beneath you. As you float, allow any lingering stress to dissolve into the calmness of the lake. Experience the serenity of weightlessness.

Picture a warm, glowing light at the centre of your chest. With each breath, feel this light expanding, radiating love and compassion. Allow this light to envelop your entire being, creating a sense of inner peace.

Open a mental door to a serene and secluded space within your mind. This space is yours, a sanctuary of peace and tranquillity. Spend a few moments enjoying the stillness and beauty of this inner retreat.

Gradually bring your awareness back to the present. Wiggle your fingers and toes, and when you're ready, gently open your eyes. Carry the sense of calm and rejuvenation with you as you navigate the rest of your day.

20. UPLIFTING FREQUENCIES

Within the realm of mindfulness, the practice of energy activation through meditation serves as a vibrant current, inviting individuals to tap into the reservoirs of positive and uplifting frequencies that reside within. Rooted in ancient wisdom and contemporary understanding of vibrational energies, these meditative practices aim to elevate one's state of being. Research in the intersection of mindfulness and energy psychology suggests that intentional engagement with uplifting frequencies can lead to increased vitality, heightened mood, and a greater sense of overall wellbeing. By directing attention towards positive and energising aspects of one's inner and outer experiences, individuals may experience a shift in consciousness, fostering a profound connection with the vibrant energies that surround and permeate existence. As we embark on the mindful exploration of energy activation, the meditation for uplifting frequencies emerges as a transformative conduit, inviting individuals to attune themselves to the harmonious vibrations that resonate with joy, inspiration, and an awakened sense of aliveness.

Celestial Elevation (3-5 minutes)

Begin by finding a quiet and comfortable space. Sit or lie down in a relaxed position. Close your eyes and take a few deep breaths to centre yourself.

Focus your attention on your breath. Inhale deeply through your nose, allowing the air to fill your lungs, and exhale slowly through your mouth. Feel the rhythm of your breath, letting it anchor you to the present moment.

Visualise a radiant sphere of light surrounding you. This light is filled with positive energy and healing vibrations. As you breathe in, imagine this light entering your body, spreading warmth and positivity to every cell.

With each exhale, release any tension or negativity. Picture it leaving your body as dark energy, dissolving into the universe. Feel a sense of lightness and clarity replacing the space where negativity once resided.

Shift your focus to gratitude. Think about things you're grateful for – big or small. Feel the warmth of gratitude filling your heart and merging with the radiant light around you. Let this positive energy amplify your vibrations.

Connect with higher energies. Imagine a beam of light extending from the top of your head, reaching up to higher realms. Visualise this connection as a channel for divine energy to flow into your being. Sense the elevated frequencies entering your body, mind, and spirit.

Repeat to yourself:

"I am a being of light."

"I am in tune with positive vibrations."

"I radiate love and joy."

Gradually bring your awareness back to the present moment. Feel the connection between your body and the earth. Picture roots extending from your being, grounding you in the present reality while carrying the elevated energies with you.

When you're ready, slowly open your eyes. Take a moment to appreciate the renewed sense of energy and positivity within you.

Remember, you can revisit this meditation whenever you feel the need to elevate your vibrations and cultivate a positive mindset.

Refreshing Energy (8-12 Minutes)

Begin by finding a comfortable and quiet space. Sit or lie down in a relaxed position. Take a moment to acknowledge the present moment and let go of any lingering thoughts.

Inhale deeply through your nose, drawing in pure, revitalising energy. As you exhale through your mouth, release any tension or stress. Feel the breath as a conduit for renewal, cleansing your mind and body.

Visualise yourself surrounded by the gentle rhythms of nature. Imagine the grounding energy of the earth beneath you, supporting and nourishing your being. Feel a sense of connection to the natural world.

Envision a radiant sun rising on the horizon. Picture its warm and golden rays cascading down upon you. As the sun's light touches your skin, sense the frequencies of warmth and positivity infusing every part of your being.

Picture a serene river of crystal-clear water. See yourself standing by its banks. Dip your hands into the water and feel its pure essence. As you do, allow the water to wash away any lingering negativity, leaving you refreshed and renewed.

Tune into the sounds around you, whether it's the rustle of leaves, birdsong, or distant waves. Let these natural sounds envelop you in a soothing symphony of frequencies. Feel each sound resonating with your inner self, elevating your vibrations.

Place your hand over your heart and focus on the rhythm of your heartbeat. With each beat, cultivate feelings of gratitude. Think about the people, experiences, and aspects of your life that bring you joy. Let gratitude amplify the frequencies of your heart. Feel that these energetic frequencies lift you to new heights.

Fuel your body with strength, resilience, and capacity to rise above challenges.

Slowly bring your awareness back to the present moment. Feel the harmony of the rising frequencies within you. As you return, carry this sense of elevated energy into your daily life.

Take a moment to reflect on the experience. Consider how the rising frequencies have transformed your inner state. Know that you can return to this meditation whenever you seek renewal and a connection to higher vibrations.

Universal Energy Activation (15 Minutes)

Begin by finding a quiet and comfortable space. Sit or lie down with your back straight and your hands resting gently on your lap. Close your eyes and take a few deep breaths, allowing yourself to settle into the present moment.

Bring your attention to your breath. Inhale deeply through your nose, feeling the air fill your lungs, and exhale slowly through your mouth, releasing any tension. With each breath, imagine a soft, golden light expanding within you, creating a serene space for your practice.

Visualise roots extending from the base of your spine, reaching deep into the earth. Feel a grounding energy as these roots connect you to the core of the planet. Sense the stability and support that Mother Earth provides.

Shift your focus to your energy centres. Begin at the base of your spine, envisioning a vibrant red light. Move upward to the sacral area, visualising an orange glow, then to the solar plexus with a yellow light. Continue through the heart (green), the throat (blue), your third eye (indigo), and the crown Chakra (violet) The crown Chakra lies at the crown of the head where the skull meets the spine. It forms a strong connection with the supreme Self. Imagine each energy centre harmonising and glowing brightly.

Picture yourself standing in a meadow bathed in soft, radiant light. As you inhale, feel the energy of the meadow rising with you. With each exhale, release any stagnant energy. Visualise the frequency of the light intensifying, creating a beautiful symphony of colours around you.

Let the vibrant energy of the soft, radiant light be now accompanied by a symphony of sounds. Imagine the melodic song of birds, the gentle rustling of leaves, and the rhythmic flow of a babbling brook in the meadow. Allow these sounds to resonate within you.

Repeat the following affirmation:

"I am in harmony with the universe."

As you affirm this, sense the resonance within you. Feel the integration of higher frequencies aligning with your physical, mental, and spiritual being.

Now, visualise yourself gently floating above the meadow, carried by the harmonious frequencies and the empowering symphony of nature. Feel the weightlessness as you rise effortlessly, connecting with the expansive sky above. With each breath, sense the meadow shrinking beneath you, providing a serene perspective of the world below.

As you float, allow any remaining tension or concerns to dissipate, like clouds drifting away. Envision yourself surrounded by a cocoon of soft, radiant light, creating a protective and comforting space. The symphony of nature continues to echo, harmonising with the gentle breeze that carries you higher.

In this elevated state, acknowledge the freedom of floating, detached from earthly worries. Embrace the tranquillity of the sky and let the currents of higher frequencies guide you towards profound serenity. Feel a profound sense of liberation and connection to the universe.

When you're ready, gently start to descend, knowing that the elevated frequencies and the empowering symphony remain within you, grounding you back into the meadow with renewed vitality and a serene heart.

Gradually bring your awareness back to the present moment. Wiggle your fingers and toes, and when you're ready, open your eyes. Take a moment to express gratitude for the experience, acknowledging the harmony you've cultivated within and around you.

ABOUT THE AUTHOR

Geraldine Bourgeon is a dedicated advocate for wellbeing, offering compassionate support to individuals navigating life's challenges. With a deep passion for spirituality, healing, and natural living, she brings a holistic approach to her work.

After completing a Master's in Applied Positive Psychology, Geraldine has worked as a life coach and trainer, specialising in guiding diverse audiences through the complexities of anxiety, stress, and various life challenges. Her commitment to empowering others has been a driving force in her career.

Drawing from decades of meditation experience, Geraldine has crafted a diverse range of materials designed to support her clients and classes. Her unique blend of expertise in positive psychology and mindfulness creates a powerful synergy that fosters personal growth and resilience.

In addition to her professional pursuits, Geraldine is an avid mindfulness practitioner, constantly seeking new ways to enhance her own wellbeing and the wellbeing of those she serves. Her commitment to mindful living is inspirational and makes her a trusted guide for those on their journey to inner peace and fulfilment.

Made in United States
North Haven, CT
18 June 2024